FROM THE AUTHOR OF "THE HOCKEY STICK PRINCIPLES"

The

Blade

Years

Bobby Martin

How 7 Successful Founders Achieved
Hockey Stick Revenue Growth

Dedicated to my family - Gloria, Jayne Beth, and Sanders.

THE BLADE YEARS

Table of Contents

Introduction   **1**

Chapter 1: Wes Aiken's Schedulefly: Starting Without   **5**
Planning

Chapter 2: Doug Lebda's LendingTree: Managing a   **29**
Good Idea So That It Morphs into a Big
Company

Chapter 3: Brian Hamilton's Sageworks: Summoning   **59**
the Grit To Keep On

Chapter 4: iContact's Ryan Allis: Using Kinetic Energy   **113**
to Create Growth

Chapter 5: Graham Snyder's SEAL Innovation: **113**
Objectifying and Transforming Frustration
into Creation

Chapter 6: My Own Start-up, First Research: Building a   **141**
Viable Company with Limited Capital

Chapter 7: Bob Young's Red Hat Software: Bringing   **173**
Forth Luck—Or Is It Skill?

Chapter 8: Evaluation   **205**

Appendix   **221**

THE BLADE YEARS

Introduction

I'm the author of *The Hockey Stick Principles: The 4 Key Stages to Entrepreneurial Success*. When writing that book, I conducted in-depth interviews of nearly a dozen successful founders. *The Blade Years* tells seven of their stories of surviving and thriving during the "Blade Years" – the stage of a start-up when founders dedicate their full-time effort to their business until it reaches revenue take-off. For most start-ups, the Blade Years last 3 or 4 years.

The details in these stories are primarily about the Blade Years, but you should be familiar with the other three stages. The first stage is Tinkering, when founders are considering their ideas before quitting their day jobs or investing a lot of money. The second stage is the Blade Years when revenue is low and not substantially growing. The third stage is the Growth Inflection Point when revenue starts taking off and when the groundwork laid during the Blade Years starts to pay off. The fourth stage is Surging Growth when management, leadership, and operational skills are so important.

But in this book, we're focusing specifically on The Blade Years. It's a precarious stage. During this time, the founder is frustrated after examining several unproductive rabbit holes and often he or she feels like a failure. "Perhaps my idea wasn't quite so good after all," the entrepreneur worries. "And now I have nothing. This venture was a mistake!" But during this stage, he or she does do necessary, thus true, work in gaining knowledge of the scope and depth of the project—and the industry. The truth is that trial and error is the only way to build a solid foundation for the start-up's learning curve.

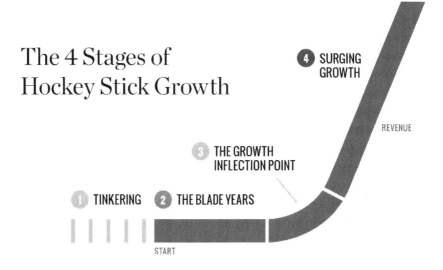

The 4 Stages of
Hockey Stick Growth

If the founder persists and if, indeed, the idea is adapted over many months into a workable, marketable one, the start-up makes a sudden revenue turn upward and hockey stick growth is obtained.

The 1979 song "Message in a Bottle," from The Police, depicts a lonely, despairing man who writes a letter, places it in a bottle, and throws it into the sea, proclaiming he'll "send an SOS to the world." Years later, the man, still alone, returns to the beach.

"Walked out this morning,
Don't believe what I saw—
A hundred billion bottles
Washed up on the shore.
Seems I'm not alone at being alone,
A hundred billion castaways
Looking for a home."[1]

Millions of potential innovative entrepreneurs face career desolation like that today. They are stuck in dead-end jobs, yet hold, like a radiant green-glass bottle, this note in their thoughts: "I desire to create and build an innovative company, but I can't overcome the risk and uncertainty of such an undertaking. SOS! What should I do?" Like the lyric singer of the song "Message in a Bottle," they are looking for an answer—some inspirational sign that gives them the trust and courage to act—to turn their lonely inaction into purposeful action. They want to motivate—but also reassure—their confidence: seeing both drive and comfort. They want to believe again in their own capacity for individual achievement that also makes a contribution.

The Blade Years is my response to the messages in bottles thrown out to sea by aspiring innovative entrepreneurs: "Help! I'm sinking under the weight of fear."

Each of the seven stories is like a personal message from a founder to answer in detail anyone who is interested in how good ideas become great companies and who needs both a push and a pat on the shoulder to start out and start up on their own.

To make the stories relevant as well as inspirational, I included background information about the founders and their product ideas so that you can see why these businesses grew as they did. I've answered these questions for you:

- What were the founder's motivation and hesitation in starting the business?
- How did he come up with the idea?
- What actions did he take first and why?
- How did he feel about having financial and business partners?
- What were the results of their financial choices?
- What were their biggest decision errors and challenges along the way?

- How did they climb up out of empty, dead-end rabbit holes and overcome their challenges? What became of their company?
- And why is that the result?

A company's start-up is like a puzzle, you need all the pieces to appreciate the entire picture. All the pieces are here. Read on to learn about seven founders' journeys, and, in particular, how the founders navigated the Blade Years and how anticipating such a growth curve graph will inspire and guide your own venture.

The stories of fits and starts are not surprising to business-writer Peter Drucker: "Classic economics…including the Keynesians, the Friedmanites, and the Supply-siders… cannot handle the entrepreneur, but consign him to the shadowy realm of 'external forces,' together with climate and weather, government and politics, pestilence and war, but also [with] technology."[2]

Having been an entrepreneur myself, and having spent much of the past four years researching other entrepreneurs, I agree with Drucker. Entrepreneurship is more of a behavior, an undying habit of trial and error, of hint - evaluate - adjust, than it is a business model.

However, I've also learned that entrepreneurship does have some best practices, such as good management, and it is good to follow them. Just because entrepreneurship is somewhat fluid, like the weather, that doesn't mean it can't be predicted with a reasonable rate of success. For example, most innovative start-ups' plotted revenue growth curves are shaped like a hockey stick. But first, you must successfully navigate the Blade Years.

Chapter 1
Wes Aiken's Schedulefly:
Starting Without Planning

Market forces influence the unique shape of any start-up's growth curve. For example, buyer-choices, pricing strategies, and market adoption play critical roles in determining growth. But market factors aren't the only determinants that shape a start-up's growth curve. A start-up's early phase focuses on the human—the founder's goals and individual style of how he or she wants to conduct business.

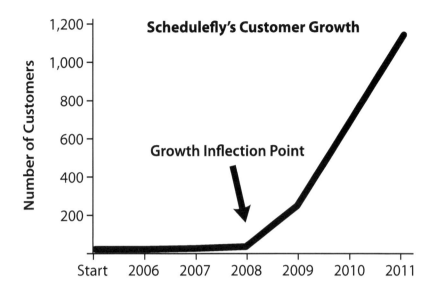

Introduction

Wes Aiken's good idea is Schedulefly, a web tool that enables independent restaurants to manage their employee work schedules online. The old, cumbersome way of announcing next week's work schedule was to pin it up on a bulletin board in the restaurant. Employees would have to phone in or drop by to get their new schedule, then copy it down, day by day. Using Schedulefly, restaurants can manage work schedules online—saving managers and employees much time and many headaches.

Schedulefly primarily serves independent restaurants so it can customize features and marketing for that segment of the market. This narrow vertical approach provides Schedulefly with focus, an advantage over the competition: online scheduling firms that market to *all* service-oriented firms, such as large restaurant chains, retail stores, fitness centers, groceries, and convenience stores.

The online scheduling market for independent restaurants is plenty big. According to Vertical IQ, there are 355,000 restaurant firms in the US. If a majority of them adopted online schedules, the market could run more than $100 million a year in the U.S. alone.

Schedulefly has five employees—three of whom are partners. Wes is the founder and software programmer; Tyler Rullman, the operations manager and strategist; and Wil Brawley, the marketer. Wes doesn't publicize Schedulefly's revenue, but it provides the partners with good income and enough left over to improve their product. Schedulefly has never sought outside capital.

Today Wes isn't programming work-schedule software. He's ratcheting line from a fly rod reel in his flatbed skiff above the marsh northwest of Wilmington, North Carolina. Wes zings a purple-feathered, red-tailed, buggish lure sixty feet to a point right between brown marsh grass and a floating stump. Tanned and hawk-eyed with prominent eyebrows, Wes's brown hair pokes in points from his camouflage fishing cap as he focuses on his target.

He's after red drum, the spangled saltwater fish often ten pounds or more that lurks in the shallows eating crabs and mullet.

"I could fish trout in the inlet, flounder in the marsh, mackerel, but I chase red drum with a fly rod, the most challenging way to fish. I could catch more by trolling bait and drinking beer with my buddies, but that's the exact opposite of why I'm out here.

"I love the quiet. It's amazing how focused your eyes and ears can become when your mouth is not moving for hours on end. I hear the osprey lifting off her nest behind me, the oyster-catchers cracking shells with their long orange beaks, the wind, the tide, and even the baitfish. Heck—chewing gum can be distracting. Being still, focused, patient, quiet, smelling and listening to the outdoors is like therapy."

Fishing for red drum, Wes is in his element.

When booking a time to fish together, Wes says, "My life revolves around the moon's pull." He's referring to the optimal time for catching red drum based upon oceanic tides. But Wes also hints that respecting the moon's cyclical, inevitable pull is how he created Schedulefly. Respecting the pace of slow, natural time passing.

Screwing Around, Making C's

Well before Wes ever thought up Schedulefly, he was twenty-two and still finding himself: "It took me a long time to figure out what I wanted to study and do. I ended up graduating from college in 1998—eight years after I graduated from high school." During his eight-year stint, Wes lived on Wrightsville Beach, North Carolina – an odd mix of surfer-dudes against a background of high-end second homes owned by wealthy North Carolinians. A part-time student, he was also a waiter at a seafood restaurant and an assistant golf pro. "I was going to school, taking a class or two and just screwing around – making Cs," he recalls.

Wes was the creative, quiet, 1990s grunge-type. One year for Halloween he dressed as "Cochese" of the rock band *Beastie Boys'* "Sabotage" music video. He stole the show at the party while maintaining his quiet, alert persona. He's quirky, but not for the shock value. Rather, Wes is understatedly different. He dresses casual, comfortable, yet GQ.

Over coffee, Wes talked old times at a cafe in Wrightsville Beach. After college he wasn't ready to grow up. "I didn't want to put on a suit and do some desk job like my friends were doing. I liked working at a restaurant. My rent was $200 a month and I'd make that in one night. You make $500 a week – cash – and then wake up on Monday morning and you don't have a dime. But you go do it again. Yeah, I was happy."

Eventually, and on his own terms, Wes discovered a computer-programming class and gravitated to it. And in 1998 he graduated from the University of North Carolina at Wilmington with an honors degree in Information Technology.

I'd Given My Baby Away, and It Felt Wrong

During the next few years of the dot-com boom, Wes worked for various technology companies, but their work approach oozed of waste and inefficiency, offending him. "My employer put me on a project in Charlotte with a company that was creating this piece of software for 401(k) tracking. A typical dot-com, they were playing foosball at three in the afternoon and working at ten at night when I was way past ready to get home.

"There was nothing appealing to me about working like that for somebody else. I remember thinking, 'This just doesn't seem productive. Hire all these people – pay them a lot of money and get this fancy office. Why don't we gather up all these people, get it done, and go home?'"

Wes wasn't one to go with the flow. He started spending a great deal of free time reading and learning about software coding, growing dedicated to the field. That's "The 10,000 Hours Rule" Malcolm Gladwell defines in his 2008 book, *Outliers*: "10,000 hours of practice is required to achieve the level of mastery associated with being a world-class expert—in anything." [3]

Gladwell adds that gifted masters like Mozart, the Beatles, and Bill Gates become obsessed with their crafts and practice incessantly; only in that way do they reach a level of brilliance. Bill Gates spent much of his time in high school doing computer programming: "It was my obsession. I skipped athletics. I went up there [to the computer center at the University of Washington] at night. We were programming on weekends." [4]

From about 1999 until 2004, like a Gladwell "Outlier," Wes was spending a tremendous amount of his free time learning software code. "At this time I wasn't thinking about products or creating something for myself, I was still learning like crazy. I would pick up a good book, or go to Barnes and Noble after a whole day working, and read about Java Software development. I read like mad for probably five years."

From about 1996, when Wes first became interested in computer programming, until 2004, he easily clocked the 10,000 hours Gladwell says it takes to become a world-class expert. Besides devouring all he could find about building software, Wes spent 2002 to 2004 bouncing from one technology job to the next – never finding satisfaction. While directing a project for the U.S. Postal Service scheduling mail pickups, his confidence increased when he recognized he could build valuable, complex, integrated turnkey systems on his own.

Tired of writing software for other people, Wes came to feel like a surrogate mother. "Because when I was done, we'd hand it over, and they'd say here's the next one. Aside from being paid well to do it, I had no investment – I'd created something but I'd given it to them. I'd given my baby away, and it felt wrong."

Wes had the itch to do his own project, but at the same time he was settling down. In 2001, he married Taylor Armstrong and they planned a family. He thought joining his parents' business, Patsy Aiken Designs, might give him the satisfaction of creating something. If the job went well, then perhaps he could take over running the business one day.

"My parents and I thought maybe we could groom me to take over their business. I learned pretty quickly that this was their baby, their business, and their life. I had a growing entrepreneurial spirit to build something, yet I was having to do it their way. It works for them, but it wasn't what I wanted to do."

In 2005 Wes stepped down from working for his parents to try something that was both *his* idea and *his* baby.

Coding Schedulefly in His Pajamas

With a desire for creation and time on his hands, plus a resis-
tance to working for other people, Wes cast around for a good idea.
"There must be some software I can create and sell," he thought.

From his college job, he was intimate with how things get
done at restaurants.

As a manager at the Bridge Tender Restaurant, in Wilmington,
N.C., what frustrated him was "having to deal with forty waiters,
all with different scheduling requests every week," he said. "On
Sunday nights, here's how it all went down: I would drive to the
restaurant five miles from my house. I would get a black book in
the office that had waiter tickets with their schedule requests: 'I
want to work here.' 'I can't work then.' Half of their requests I
couldn't even read! So I would drive home and have to call them
all.

"I'd create a schedule on paper, then drive back to the restaurant to hang the schedule up." It was a typical restaurant's weekly
scheduling process, yet Wes saw it as highly inefficient. Soon, he
figured that *this* might be his idea, his problem to work on and try
to solve. Could scheduling servers at the Bridge Tender be better
managed online with an easy-to-use software system?

Once Wes decided to pursue his idea, his approach contradicted
the advice in just about every How-to-Start-Your-Own-Business
book. He went deep into building the software, ignoring everything else. No business plan, no investors, no banks, no partners,
no due diligence, no planning, no market research, no surveying
potential customers, and, best of all, no drama:

"There were no official software requirements. There were no
meetings beforehand with other developers or shareholders or investors. There was no money. There was no discussion about out
how the system would be architected, where it would live, how it

would scale to thousands of users. There was no plan.

"I was just a guy in pajamas with a laptop, writing a simple system I thought restaurants might like. No bigger than that. It was so clear that I could help restaurants with a really simple system. I knew how to write software and I had a concrete example of a business problem that needed fixing.

"I sat in my house for four or five months in my underwear and when it was cold, my pajamas, and created the first version of Schedulefly—purely from remembering what I had to do to make our Bridge Tender schedule happen."

Wes didn't seriously consider how he'd sell or market his idea. His approach wasn't much different from Mark Zuckerberg's in starting Facebook. According to the film *The Social Network*, Mark got the idea for Facebook from what classmates said they needed, then day and night for weeks he buried himself in his dorm room and coded the program.[5] Zuckerberg didn't consider marketing or how to monetize his idea. He just knew the idea was cool and figured that others would appreciate it. Marketing and monetizing would take care of themselves: if you build it, they will come.

Programming the first version of his online restaurant scheduling system took Wes roughly five months. He worked long hours, grew a beard, and buried himself in his room, coding SQL and .NET code.

When he finished it, Wes called his product Schedulefly because of his love for red drum fly fishing. "Yeah, and I remember people telling me, 'You should name it, like, ScheduleFast or ScheduleQuick or something.' But those names were too corporate and sounded like any other company's.

"I just liked that word Schedulefly. I remember asking my parents about the fly-fishing aspect of it. They liked it. And I envisioned the schedule 'flying,' you know, out on the Web, not hanging on a wall. So the name stuck. And now, in hindsight, it's a much more brandable name than others people suggested. I see that every day."

With a name and a workable program, Wes asked a few of his friends' restaurants—an Italian restaurant and a casual pizza place—to try out Schedulefly, though he cautions, "I didn't have a business yet. I had a software product."

Schedulefly Takes a Hiatus

What happened next? Hardly anything. For two years, from 2005 until 2007, Wes's working restaurant employee scheduling system quietly ran on a server in his closet at home while two restaurants enjoyed using it.

In 2005, Wes did, however, convince his cousin Mark, a graphic artist, to design Schedulefly some marketing materials. "I did one thing that I kind of regret," Wes said. "I spent, like, fourteen hundred bucks creating a handout kind of thing in a nice folder. Those marketing folders sat in my closet and collected dust for a couple of years. And finally, when we moved, I was, like, 'Oh, my God! Look at these things!' I never did anything with them. There were like a thousand of them; I just tossed them. Totally wish I'd bought a new fly rod instead of spending fourteen hundred dollars on those stupid handouts."

During most of those two years Wes worked for my own company, First Research. I had known about Wes's reputation for building scalable software systems, so I begged him to join our team and made him a hard-to-refuse offer. He accepted and joined First Research.

I later asked Wes why he took my offer instead of pursuing Schedulefly. "Timing wasn't right. I hated selling and had no one to help me think about how to sell it. I also had no money."

He didn't try raising money or finding a partner because he had no interest or experience in either gambit. "Raising money to finance Schedulefly never crossed my mind," he said. "What would I do with money? What would they be investing in? Nah. I needed money for the Aiken family—not for Schedulefly. I had no one to help me sell the software and run the business. Honestly, at that time I never planned for it to be a real business. I never dreamed it would be where it is today."

Wes built a sophisticated, scalable software system for First Research, and left Schedulefly on autopilot: "I didn't touch it for a year; not a line of code, nothing," he recalls. "A few restaurants were using it. They'd send me a little note every once in a while to fix a bug or something. It ran in a closet next to a broom at my house."

While Schedulefly sat working in his closet, Wes was shaping his perspectives on business while working at First Research. He watched First Research struggle to manage its growth. The pressures natural to growth forced First Research to become more like an institution, rather than an original creation. He noticed that time and resources began drifting away from attracting and serving customers and into other concerns.

"First Research became about budgets. Carolyn, the controller, handed me the budget for our department one day. I saw then that when it's more about budgets and less about getting stuff done, it's not as much fun."

When we sold First Research to a larger competitor, Wes became disenchanted with having to manage people and processes. He was cynical about the practices of the big business, especially the complexity that comes along with growth.

Wes didn't care for corporate glad-handing, either. The acquiring company noticed Wes's programming talent and asked him to help with their complex technology, but he would have none of it: "When my boss came to town, he took me to Starbuck's, and he started talking all this big, 'I want you to come in and help run the software development team. I've got 80 people.' Most people would probably be like, 'Wow, great!' But it made me sick to my stomach. I just told him, 'Man, look. I'm not that guy. I'm not going to jump in and start helping you.'"

Wes believes that big businesses mostly "provide jobs" and that those jobs are "just an existence." He made fun of their spending so much time in meetings. "It seems like once a business gets big enough, the pace of innovation and growth slows because people are meeting all the time," he said. "If you had a company and told everyone, 'Work from home, don't drive to the office, don't stop by Dunkin' Donuts for the morning meeting, don't walk around and check in at every cubicle to get a status report—instead stay in your pajamas till four in the afternoon,' you wouldn't believe how fast your business would innovate and grow. This is precisely the reason I don't want an office, a water cooler, and a fridge. Especially I don't want places for people to stand around and meet."

Enter Tyler Rullman, Businessman

In the summer of 2007, a few months after First Research was sold, Wes again became anxious about his career. One of First Research's key employees was Tyler Rullman. Tyler, a thoughtful strategist and man of few words, had already played a pivotal role in helping First Research grow and succeed. He was a star basketball player at Harvard and went on to play professional basketball in Europe. Later Tyler earned an M.B.A. from UCLA. Wes and Tyler had worked together closely at First Research, so they knew well each other's personalities and goals.

Wes asked Tyler's opinion of Schedulefly. "After First Research sold, I remember I showed it to Tyler and he did his raise-an-eyebrow, barely-move 'Hmmm......' response. Nothing came of it, and he didn't mention it again."

But a few months later, Tyler made an "once-in-a-lifetime" overture to Wes about Schedulefly. "After First Research sold and Tyler decided to leave, I'll never forget it," Wes recalls. "He came and sat in my office at First Research and in typical Tyler fashion, no beating around the bush, he just said, 'Man, I think I want to help you. I think I want to run this business. Do you think it's ready for us to go and sell it to people?' And I was just blown away.

"I remember telling him, 'Hell no, it's not ready to sell to people! Look, Schedulefly has no paying customers...not one. The two guys in Raleigh who use it aren't *paying*.'"

Wes was still concerned about Schedulefly's prospects of becoming a real business because he had tried marketing it word-of-mouth yet nothing was happening. But Tyler decided to take a risk, give it a shot. He liked working in small companies, and he was in a financial position to work without pay. He had earned a substantial sum on the sale of First Research, and his wife, Teresa, had a stable corporate job.

Now that Tyler and Wes would be partners, how would they organize Schedulefly? Who would own Schedulefly's shares? How would salaries be paid? Who does what? And for how long? What might happen, and when? While Wes discovered the idea and created the product, he hadn't yet made it a real business and had no desire to do so himself: "I had a job and a salary and I wasn't going to be able to put a whole lot of effort into this.

"Whereas Tyler was going to put a full-time effort into trying to figure Schedulefly out. So we came to an agreement that kept me majority shareholder in the business but made him fired up enough to work hard. I wrote the software, but in terms of the business, he makes decisions just as important as I do."

Wes and Tyler split up Schedulefly's stock sixty-forty percent, respectively. "That happened pretty quickly," Wes remembers. "I didn't go home to hem and haw over it. I just said, 'It's either going to be a business or it's not going to be a business. And I'm not going to do it on my own. You went to Harvard and you helped grow First Research.' So there was never a second of doubt in either of our minds that this wasn't the right scenario."

Twenty Months of Trial and Error

From September 2007 until May 2009 Tyler was Schedulefly's only nine-to-five employee. During that time, Wes moonlighted coded improvements for Schedulefly on nights and weekends, but during the day he worked for First Research.

Tyler wrestled with how to market and sell Schedulefly. He thought selling it door-to-door was a bad idea. "I wasn't going to sell door-to-door because it's not my nature and it's embarrassing," Tyler says. "And I just didn't think it was going to work to get us to any kind of scale. You might get a one-off here or there, but you're approaching dozens of people and burning up gas, burning up time in getting to know people . . . it's just not worth it."

Tyler believed he could attract more customers via the Internet with free trial offers. The first three months would be free, and then after the trial period, a restaurant could convert to paying $39 per month for Schedulefly. Customers could cancel at any time.

Tyler initiated two tactics: website optimization and email marketing.

Schedulefly tweaked the website to get it ready for online commerce and invested $1,500 per month into Internet advertising. And Tyler started an email campaign designed to get free trials. Sitting in front of a computer for hundreds of hours, he devoted himself to mind-boggling grunt work. Even if the emails got a low response rate, he figured a few restaurants might accept free trials—valuable for getting people "into the system."

"In October I emailed thousands of restaurants," Tyler said. "You know, when you spend a month, every night and all night long, sending emails and you're getting two or three customers, it's like, 'Oh, God, c'mon!'"

By March of 2008, Internet advertising and the email campaign had produced roughly twenty restaurants, each paying them $39 per month—that's only $800 per month, hardly enough to pay the light bill. It was small potatoes, though something. More important, Schedulefly now had customers to give them feedback that would lead to enhancements and features helpful in getting more customers.

Cruel to be Kind

Nick Lowe's 1979 song "Cruel to be Kind" is about relationships, but it could also pertain to entrepreneurship.[6] Rejection by potential or actual customers may feel cruel when you receive it, but it's kind in that it helps a start-up unearth and then properly adjust to real customer demands. Cruel really can be kind in the long run, and Schedulefly learned in detail how to improve their product from the details of each rejection.

Free-trial customers were often hard on Tyler when he asked why Schedulefly had failed to meet their needs. "When you introduce something that's totally different, they're either going to get it and say, 'Wow, this is cool; it makes my life a lot easier.' Or they're going to say, 'This isn't how I did it before; I only know how to do it one way. You must be an idiot! You don't know how we do scheduling in the restaurant industry.' I got yelled at a lot."

But Wes and Tyler didn't view the yelling as insults, they viewed it as free feedback to help them develop enhancements that would improve future free-trial conversion rates. "The people who signed up for trials but did not convert, which was most of them, were sometimes brutally honest, and that kind of feedback was usually more helpful than what we heard from folks who liked us."

They made several improvements to the system based on the feedback from the restaurants that didn't convert. Schedulefly software's first version was missing some elements. For example, it lacked a time-off feature that enabled restaurant employees to use Schedulefly to request time off, be approved, and have another employee pick up their shift. Creating the time-off software was a mentally exhausting, yet stimulating process that Wes and Tyler worked on together for several days straight. "We laugh about the [difficulty of our time-off project]," Wes recalls. "Tyler came down to Wilmington and stayed for three days at my parents' house. We sat at the kitchen table and designed how this time-off system would work, down to the very SQL statements that I had to write to get the data in the system. It was a huge addition to what we could offer, but a monster."

The "cruel-to-be-kind" feedback was working, because the product improved. But Schedulefly needed more customers to generate enough cash to pay salaries for Tyler and Wes. Tyler searched for new ways to market Schedulefly. He tried online blogging that got them nowhere; they joined restaurant associations … another goose egg; they tried direct mail… not much there. And he tried some out-of-the-box ideas. For example, while his selling door-to-door was out of the question, Tyler did try commission-only sales:

"Another experiment was to advertise on Craig's List for people in college towns like Tallahassee, Gainesville, or Columbia, S.C., to sell and work on commission to spread the word about Schedulefly—the thinking here was that college towns have a high concentration of young workers who are open to technology and usually a lot of restaurants and bars to serve them. We learned a couple of things—first, that the economics from a commission standpoint are a joke. The student sales corps found out that they would have to call on 100 people to make a sale—and it ended quickly. Lesson learned for them—and for us."

Tyler realized that trying different approaches was just part of the process, not a sign of failure. "Getting something off the ground from nothing and doing that by yourself is real hard—you'll try anything to get it done," he said.

He was keen that word-of-mouth could be a powerful, low-cost marketing. Small, innovative, entrepreneurial businesses often distinguish themselves by surprising customers through their service and unflagging attention, and that good news spreads like rumor among their business sector.

Converting the Masses

"There's no really easy way to market to restaurants because the industry is just so fragmented," Tyler said. "But I knew that they are the kind of community that talks to each other. I took really good care of the customers that we got—answering calls at midnight, that kind of thing. They had a lot of questions; they had a lot of problems. But they always got somebody here to answer the phone or to respond within a few minutes. So, I knew that [growing Schedulefly] was probably going to be a matter of word-of-mouth because it's really hard to reach independent restaurants."

Word-of-mouth marketing didn't work well immediately, though. It took years for it to make a noticeable impact. "I thought when we had one restaurant in each city, then they'd start talking. But it takes longer than that. It takes thousands of workers in each city just to get one or two more customers, and then it snowballs on top of that."

Another marketing experiment was trying public relations,

Schedulefly promoting itself to magazine and trade editors. If an editor is impressed with the solution, they may write an article about the idea.

So instead of taking salaries, Wes and Tyler invested their scant revenue into hiring a marketing firm to promote them to the media with press releases and editorial pitches. That strategy worked. An editor from *Nations Restaurant News (NRN)* noticed how helpful Schedulefly could be, and put them on its front page.

"To be put in *Nations Restaurant News* was probably one of the biggest things that ever happened to us," Tyler said. "It's like the bible for the restaurant industry. And tens of thousands—if not hundreds of thousands—of people read it. So to be able to put that on your Website was huge. We were getting people to come in and look at our site through the optimization and the Internet advertising; we just weren't getting that many of them to convert, because by then a few other online scheduling sites were out there. In any case, the *NRN* mention did improve our conversion rates."

Enter Wil Brawley, Sales and Marketing Energy

By the middle of 2008, more than three years after Wes created the first version of Schedulefly, the company was beginning to hit its growth inflection point. The various reasons for rejection had educated them, and they had tweaked the product to the point of its being easy to use and intuitive. The number of free trials was rising and the conversion rates were increasing from five percent, to ten, and now closing in on twenty percent. And customers almost never dropped it once they'd fully implemented Schedulefly.

Tyler was wearing multiple hats managing customer service, product strategy, administrative support, and finance. Furthermore, he was spending a greater portion of his time marketing and selling. Soon he couldn't do a good job in every area.

Wes and Tyler pondered what was next for Schedulefly. Perhaps they could market and sell Schedulefly to larger restaurant chains. But doing so would require in-person, highly-skilled selling, travel, and lots of focus. Tyler had no desire to sell. His skills and career aspirations were best suited to product and business strategy, operations, finance, and marketing.

Wil Brawley had been a star salesman and partner at First Research. Wes and Tyler knew him well and felt comfortable with his approach to business. Like Wes and Tyler, he enjoyed hobbies, family, and friends more than working seventy hours a week. And Wil was in a financial position to work patiently without a salary, or for a small salary, until Schedulefly grew enough to pay him. An affable salesman, Wil lives to make customers happy. He's jovial, outgoing, passionate, competitive, challenge-seeking, high-octane, fun, and interesting. Wil was the perfect fit for Schedulefly.

"Wil came down here to Wilmington one weekend to fish and talk, and to see if Schedulefly was something he might consider. He was considering some other opportunities, too," Wes recalls.

Wes and Tyler offered to make Wil a minority shareholder in Schedulefly, but the three structured compensation as if all three were equal partners. With a simple formula, everyone gets the same pay. "We would figure out how much money we needed to save for the business, and then we would pay each other the same out of the remainder, increasing our salaries as we grew. We just said, look, we're in this together. We think [parity is] the right plan because it gets everybody fired up to work hard at it—motivation was the main point."

Wil accepted their offer, rounding out the team's skills. "This is when I really started to get excited," Wes said. "Adding Wil was a key third piece. We had me to work on the product; Tyler to focus on strategy, operations, and product advice. And now Wil would focus on how to get Schedulefly out there."

Wil joined Schedulefly in October 2008 to focus on creating a buzz with independent restaurants. Wes wanted to stick with small restaurants because his past work had been in indies. They were wise to focus on that expanding niche, it turns out. Wil brought more than social-media savvy to the business; he had a genial, outgoing energy that the two founders didn't. His talent for working with the public has contributed to Schedulefly's recent success.

"Because I'm introverted, the most I'll do is send an email, you know?" Tyler said. "I'm not going to call anybody. But Wil, he'll be on the phone all day long calling everybody, and he won't rest until he talks to them and convinces them to buy our stuff, or at least try us."

Today Schedulefly is a trifecta: Wes the programmer, Tyler the strategist, and Wil the marketer—a good formula. Not surprisingly, Schedulefly took off in 2009. It doesn't publish revenues, but it is more than just a viable operation now.

Where Are They Now

In 2016, Wes still owns a majority of Schedulefly, an established leader in restaurant scheduling software. Free trials pour in and conversion rates are high. It boasts 6,300 restaurants as customers and still is growing fast.

With some longevity and experience in working together, Schedulefly has developed a personality. Not surprisingly, it mirrors Wes's independent nature. His approach to managing Schedulefly is much like that illustrated in the best-selling, entrepreneurial know-how book *Rework*, by Jason Fried and David Hansson. Full of edgy advice about how to create a company, some of the book's tenets are: "Planning is guessing," "Fire the workaholics," "Why grow?" "Let your customers outgrow you," "Ignore the real world," "Building to flip is building to flop," "Send people home at 5," "Forget about formal education," "Outside money is plan Z," and "Pass on great people."[7]

Wes has adopted many of the post-millennial business philosophies from *Rework* applicable to lifestyle software companies. One example of Wes's free-spirited approach to managing Schedulefly is not hiring a PR firm to promote the company. Since Wes considers conventional PR firms predictable, expensive, and "corporate," Schedulefly markets its services in its own way. For example, Wil has created dozens of videos of restaurant owners telling their stories and offering clever advice. Schedulefly gives the videos away for free – hardly advertising their brand with the exception of a small logo in the corner of the page.

For Wes's goals, that works well. Other examples of unabashed flair are everywhere. The partners still show great abandon—the innocence and energy of youth. Schedulefly's Website offers casual videos of waiters and waitresses in their own restaurants commenting, "I love Schedulefly because my schedule comes right to my mobile phone. It's really cool!" Then restaurant employees giggle, clearly happy that setting their weekly work schedule is no longer a hassle. Schedulefly's marketing choice here is fresh, innovative, and convincingly unrehearsed. They also give away trucker hats when the mood strikes them.

Another example of creative marketing is Wil's book, *Restaurant Owners Uncorked*. Wil interviewed several software customers and transcribed their stories of starting and owning a small restaurant into a book full of knowledge and wisdom gained. The book helps and entertains the reader, but it's another attention-getting tactic, too, cementing the relationship between Schedulefly and its customers—independent restaurants.

Schedulefly's blog boasts about its lack of offices. "We do not have a lot of overhead and fancy offices, so we can invest the money we make today back into our product. We're really small, simple, excellent, and proud of it. Do business with us if you like those things."

Schedulefly's rare board meetings take place in a customer's restaurant or on Wes's fishing boat. Each of the three partners lives in a different city and works from home. Which of the three partners is in charge? I doubt it matters. They loosely divide up the responsibilities, and adjust as needed.

Schedulefly works the way Wes fishes. "We work wherever we want to work and whenever we feel inspired," he says. "Inspiration is critically important. We enjoy alone time and we work best in quiet places." Their hours have nothing to do with 8 to 5 but everything to do with when customers need them.

Schedulefly's growth prospects are enormous. With nearly three hundred thousand independent restaurants in the U.S. alone, if Schedulefly obtains even a 5% market share, it will have over 15,000 customers. How do you manage 15,000 customers and hundreds of thousands of users? Can you do it while working from home? Can you do it without managers? Can you do it without meetings?

Wes doesn't want the limitations he's put on the business to lead to stagnation, but he doesn't want to grow big, either, and that volatile state of conflicting values may be the context in which he has to find his answers.

Conclusion
In which the moon's pull guides an entrepreneur's business choices

So what's next for Schedulefly when it has 15,000 customers? How about 50,000 customers? What will Wes do with any excess cash flow? How many additional employees will Wes hire?

Here's what he says to that: "Dude, your and my experiences

and philosophies in the business world are so drastically different. You're making it complicated—which I hate."

Wes's frank retort to his old boss at First Research is telling. He won't over analyze the future. He won't worry about complexities that haven't occurred yet. He wants to make customers happy while living his life free of corporate nonsense. He lives his life according to the moon's pull on the tides that govern the behavior of coastal fisheries. By design, Wes has cut back to a bare minimum his own scheduling, analysis, and any stressful, complicated efforts at competing so he can pursue the elusive red drum.

Conventional wisdom leads us to believe that entrepreneurship is synonymous with careful, diligent planning. For example, the reference section of a public library near my home displays a bright yellow and black traffic sign with an arrow pointing straight ahead: "How to Start Your Own Business – For Entrepreneurs." Book titles there include *Common Sense Business, How to Run a Thriving Business, 12 Elements of Great Managing, Please I'd Rather Manage Myself, Small Time Operator, Buying a Business to Secure Your Financial Freedom,* and *Start Your Own Business.* One book contains seven hundred pages of advice for setting up financial statements, paying taxes, selling, marketing, and even how to set up credit-card processing. These books imply that business skills and following a tested plan are the most important requirements for creating an innovative business. Thumbing through the pages of these books, I found that most of the advice is contrary to the way in which Wes has built Schedulefly. The books emphasize planning and business execution.

Wes's story shows that traditional, by-the-book business knowledge is not always required of the founder to create an innovative, profitable company.

Growth-oriented entrepreneurs raise capital and gain market share as quickly as possible. But when Wes considers raising capital to gain more customers quickly and make his share of Schedulefly worth more money, he responds without hesitation: "We would be selling the business and then have to answer to some guy in a pressed dress shirt with a smart phone always emailing us asking us to do things we do not want to do. No way—I'd rather be a fishing guide and fade away into the sunset than do that."

Wes is convinced that small is good because it supports happiness. "There is no fat, no bullshit, no interruptions—just flat-out productive days," he says. "I'm innovating like mad. I get up and work quietly from about 7:30 a.m. until lunch. I mix in a run, bike, surfing, or fishing. I usually work for a few hours later on but sometimes not. I have huge spurts of uninterrupted productive time every single day."

In managing growth, Wes will have to balance realism and idealism. He faces an entrepreneurial paradox waiting in the wings: the skills required to conceive and start a venture are not the same skills needed to manage it after it's successful. As Joe Colopy, founder and CEO of multi-million-dollar Bronto Software that provides email marketing solutions, explains, "To grow a business from $0 to $100,000, or maybe even $1 million, you have to be a true entrepreneur. But to grow a business from $1 million to $10 million, you have to be an executive. At about $1 million I stopped being a real entrepreneur."

How will Wes manage this inevitable growth? Will he sell Schedulefly when it becomes more complex? Will he figure out a way to keep lots of customers happy despite having few employees? Will he keep creating brilliant software and allow his partners to manage growth complexities? Will he become an executive, a manager?

Whatever he decides, Wes will manage growth according to a plan that fits his life and personal aspirations. He likely won't be pressured into following any "plan" or "corporate strategy."

Wes isn't alone in desiring to own a lifestyle company instead of a growth company. The 2008 Panel Study of Entrepreneurship II (PSED II) was a joint effort between leading researchers to gain insight into how companies are created. The study identified and interviewed 1,214 nascent entrepreneurs. Only 22.1% of the entrepreneurs surveyed desired a company that "maximizes growth." The balance, 77.9%, desired "to grow to a size that is easy to manage." [8]

When I exchange emails with Wes, Schedulefly's business performance rarely is a topic of our conversation. Instead, his emails tell stories of catching red drum:

"We caught three fish that night. One popped up, and I missed him. Another, missed him too. Then a third—and I got him! Catching one fish is a great night. Seriously, one fish! That's all it takes. Watching red drum eat never gets old. When I cast the fly in the right spot, I literally stop breathing until he either eats it or spooks and takes off.

"I'm obsessed beyond repair."

Schedulefly's success story shows that building an innovative company can be as simple as following our heart's aspiration, instead of allowing society to define and shape our business creation for us, then having to exist within those bounds.

Chapter 2
Doug Lebda's LendingTree: Managing a Good Idea So That It Morphs into a Big Company

Startups' hockey stick-shaped growth curves are like acorns—each the seed of a mighty oak, but each possessing its own characteristics, no two the same. For example, some good ideas spend the first five years generating almost no revenue, and then explode in growth over the next five years. Doug Lebda's story of creating LendingTree reveals, however, that turning a good idea into a huge success requires more than just the *idea* itself.

Introduction

LendingTree, known for its TV and radio tagline, "When banks compete, you win," is the leading online mortgage broker. In 2015, publicly traded LendingTree, generated $254 million in revenue.

LendingTree's website makes it easy for consumers to connect with multiple lenders. Instead of physically going to a bank and applying for a loan, borrowers complete a loan request form at LendingTree.com. Based on the applicant's profile, Lending-Tree invites lenders on its network to compete for the borrower's business. Borrowers win because they have more choices, receive competitive, customized offers at no cost to them, and fill out less paperwork. Banks win because they get to connect with highly targeted borrowers they otherwise wouldn't have access to. Lending-Tree wins because the lenders pay the company a fee for matching them with borrowers.

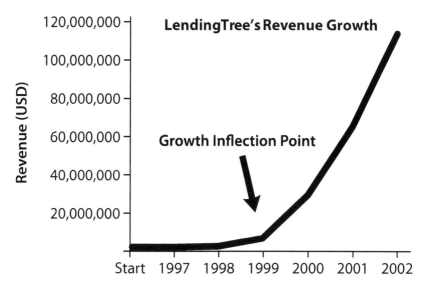

LendingTree's founder and current CEO is 45-year-old Doug Lebda. When interviewed at LendingTree's suburban Charlotte headquarters, Lebda showed a wistful nostalgia in his stories of starting LendingTree from a second bedroom. He was at ease—the kind of guy to watch football with at a bar. Doug's a tanned, trim athlete, in blue jeans and black button-down shirt for taking time today to look back and see how he and LendingTree got here, now.

The average oak tree produces thousands of acorns each year, but only one in ten thousand acorns will germinate and grow into a mighty oak tree.[9] Most acorns are consumed or destroyed by insects or animals. And poor soil conditions often prohibit germination. Finally, those that do germinate in a dense forest lack adequate light to grow.

Blue Jays and squirrels carry some of the acorns out of the dark forest and into an open, light meadow. A few of these acorns germinate and grow into tiny saplings. A few tiny saplings survive predators such as deer, harsh weather, and competition with other plant species. A strong few become mighty oak trees.

Entrepreneurship works the same as the acorn-to-mighty-oak life cycle: only a tiny percentage of good ideas become large, solid, recognizable companies. Most good ideas don't become businesses at all—they just stew in the mind of their inventor, the best of them lucky enough to be discussed over a beer or a glass of wine among friends. The few good ideas that do become businesses often don't survive, or they remain small, niche, lifestyle businesses by design, inaction, distraction, financial difficulties, or for other reasons.

For example, my business partner Ingo's son, Matt, told me about his idea to create a new kind of social network. His idea was a site like Facebook, but only close friends could befriend one another and share content. I could see it was a great way to continue meaningful friendships. But Matt's good idea foundered despite some financial support.

"Matt had a really good idea, but having a really good idea isn't good enough," Ingo said. "You have to figure out how to implement it—then drive, drive, drive to get it done. Matt set out his idea more than five years ago, but, crucially, he lacked a partner with business experience who could help him turn it into a reality."

Another entrepreneur, Amanda, came up with a good idea of selling lists of qualified babysitters to parents, SitterConnection. Her idea has growth potential, but she's content to manage it as a small, lifestyle business without employees. "I don't want to grow," Amanda told me. "If SitterConnection grows, then it's going to be a different business. I'd have to get an iPhone and have it on while I'm sitting on the beach. I don't want the aggravation."

I spoke recently to a group of university business students about the start-up challenges of entrepreneurship. I described four entrepreneurial businesses, one of which was Amanda's. The other three entrepreneurs have larger established businesses. I asked the business students: "Which one of these four entrepreneurs do you most aspire to become?" Of the 30 diverse students in the classroom, 26 of them chose Amanda.

Most of us are like Amanda. We don't want the complexity, stress, and difficult problem-solving that comes with creating a big, high-growth company that relies on continual tech upgrades. Faced with any or a combination of those difficulties, many start-ups do not thrive robustly after germination. Some even wither away before they evolve into growing businesses. Doug Lebda's good idea, however, did beat the overwhelming odds, growing and surviving, becoming a mighty oak.

Doug: Master of Reality

As a twelve-year-old growing up near Lewisburg, Pennsylvania, Doug Lebda and his friends circumvented the Bucknell Golf Club's rules against retrieving and selling members' golf balls. "You're not supposed to be swimming in the golf course pond," Doug said. "So we used to sneak out of the house in the middle of the night and fish for golf balls. We'd walk around in the muddy bottom and find them with our feet or submerge, go under water, and pick them up and put them in a sock. We'd go home, clean them up, and sell them the next day."

As a high school student, Doug and his cousin sold fireworks to make money—buying them in bulk, breaking them into smaller packets, and selling them for a profit. Doug also cut grass and had other odd jobs to earn money to buy new snow skis. These experiences taught him self-reliance. "In those early years, I learned about eating what you kill, so to speak. And if you didn't do well, you ...," shrugging his shoulders, implying that you didn't eat.

Doug attended Bucknell, a private liberal-arts college in the rolling hills of central Pennsylvania. Despite his youthful entrepreneurial experiences, he studied accounting, and becoming an entrepreneur hardly crossed his mind. "Mine is not your crazy entrepreneurial story," he said. "I was planning to go to corporate America."

After his 1992 graduation, PriceWaterhouse hired Doug as a staff accountant. He recalls he wasn't the best accountant there, but he "worked hard and learned a lot."

Irish playwright and co-founder of the London School of Economics George Bernard Shaw writes, "Geniuses are masters of reality."[10] Brilliance often comes from seeing the world as it is, and then refusing to rest in acceptance of it—mastering it instead. Some of the most notable game-changing business ideas come from "masters of reality," those whom we least expect are innovative. One might expect a master of reality to be an industry insider, a senior manager intimate with how his or her industry works. But, paradoxically, industry insiders aren't often the ones who innovate their own industry.

For example, in a term paper he wrote at Yale, Fred Smith conceived the idea of FedEx as competition for the U.S. Postal Service. Michael Dell shipped his first custom-made computer in 1984 at 19 from his Texas college dorm room. In 1950 Howard Head invented the first metal skis because during his first ski lesson, the wooden skis performed poorly. In 1976, Head invented the Prince Oversized tennis racquet because he didn't often hit the sweet spot when he played with a traditional racquet.[11]

And Doug Lebda, a twenty-four-year-old accountant, invented a new way to apply for loans though he had no banking or technology experience whatsoever.

Doug didn't conjure up LendingTree in a sudden epiphany but mulled over his idea for a couple of years. "There was no single moment where I can remember the idea coming to me," Doug recalls. "I thought it up . . . probably from '95 'til '97. By 1997 the concept was solid, but up until that point it was evolving."

The idea came from Doug's "putting together two totally different things." In 1994 when buying a $55,000 condominium in Pittsburgh, he noticed that the mortgage application process was impractical and burdensome. "I hated the process," Doug recalls. "I was fairly savvy financially, but I thought this process sucked." The loan process took him three months to complete, costing him countless phone calls. Then right before closing, out of the blue he learned that he had to buy flood insurance.

Doug's lousy mortgage experience took root in his mind like a germinating acorn. Almost two years later, in 1996, while investigating natural gas derivatives for PriceWaterhouse, he discovered the second clue. "PriceWaterhouse had asked me to become an expert on financial derivatives," Doug recalled. "I spent time with energy traders, natural gas traders, and oil traders, watching people trade what's called 'basis' in the natural gas industry—a price differential between two locations. So if gas sells for two bucks in Charlotte, and a buck-fifty in Philadelphia, that fifty-cent price difference fluctuates, and you can actually trade that on a derivative exchange."

Doug wondered, if there were markets for so many other tradable products, like cotton and pork bellies, why wasn't there one for consumer mortgages? "It didn't make sense that you should have a local mortgage market where you apply to one provider and get rejected. It seemed to me that you should be able to have an efficient trading exchange for mortgages, just like you have for anything else."

A Second-Bedroom Operation

Early in 1996 Doug collaborated on his mortgage-exchange idea with a friend, Jamey Bennett. Jamey had started a company called Bookwire that provided online news and information about the book-publishing business. Bookwire was an innovative concept when Internet commerce was in its infancy. Doug and Jamey thought that the Internet might also be a good place for a "mortgage exchange."

Online they could advertise to consumers and offer them mortgages from multiple banks, not just one provider. They envisioned a virtual online mortgage broker. After casual conversations, Doug and Jamey each invested $1,500 and formed an equal partnership called Lewisburg Ventures, named for Bucknell's college town, Lewisburg, Pennsylvania.

From January until June 1996, Doug moonlighted and learned as much as he could about banking. He remembers being a fish out of water. "I didn't know anything about the mortgage business; I didn't know anything about banking; I didn't know anything about the Internet or technology. I mean, I literally knew nothing. I had to learn it all from scratch."

They called their product "Bankwire," like Jamey's "Bookwire," and used most of their $3,000 investment to print brochures to appear credible while pitching their idea to banks. Even though he had no product, Doug cold-called banks after researching their Chief Marketing Officers' names and contact information at the local library.

His business model was set up as a win/win, both for the consumer and for the bank, offering applicants more choices while requiring less paperwork up front. Banks would be offered more lending opportunities.

The process worked like this: Consumers fill out a loan request on Bankwire's website. Bankwire electronically delivers the application to participating banks. If the application meets the bank's pre-determined underwriting criteria (credit score, geography, income, etc.), then it bids on the application. The consumer gets back multiple rates and terms. The winning or chosen bank closes the loan directly with the consumer. Bankwire earns money when the bank pays it a small fee ($10) for the opportunity to bid on an application and $500 if and when the loan closes.

Doug figured that banks would clamor for his idea, but they were only "intrigued." For several months, he met with banks but got nowhere. "We had a lot of 'Good-Meeting Syndrome.' We'd have a good meeting…. another follow-up meeting…another meeting. They'd have to do due diligence. They didn't say 'yes' or 'no.' I assumed it would be like selling somebody a set of knives. You show up and you sell them because they're either interested or they're not." But that's not how it worked.

In one meeting with a bank, Doug discovered that the name "Bankwire" was already taken when a banker asked, "BankWire? Does that sound familiar?" His colleague exclaimed: "Yeah, that's the name of the Federal Funds Transfer System!"

Embarrassed by the snafu, Doug and Jamey changed its name to CreditSource USA.

In June of 1996, six months after incorporating Lewisburg Ventures, Doug resigned from PriceWaterhouse to pursue CreditSource USA while studying for an M.B.A. at the University of Virginia. He and his wife, Tara Garrity, settled in a tiny apartment in Charlottesville, Virginia.

CreditSource USA became a second-bedroom operation.

Doug made sales calls on banks and tried to raise capital while Tara managed a growing list of details— being licensed in every state as a mortgage broker was one.

Doug endured a "constant round-the-clock grind," attending classes from eight to one, working on CreditSource USA from one to six, and studying from six to midnight. Doug and Tara scraped by. "I bet we were living on a thousand bucks a month," Doug says. "I still remember Tara calling me from Office Depot, asking if she could buy a paper cutter."

Doug was stalling in getting his idea off the ground, though. After almost a year of trying, he didn't have great interest from the banks partly because he had no product and therefore no proof that any consumers would come to his website. Nor did he have any working technology. For example, assuming consumers did visit his website, how would the bank receive the data? How would CreditSource actually work?

If Doug was serious about his idea, then he needed to build a product and market it to consumers. And that would cost money. Since Doug didn't have much money himself, he'd have to find it. Whether to grow or stay small was never an issue for him— growth was always part of the plan.

Chasing Capital...Round One of Ten

Acorns need water to grow into mighty oak trees. Similarly, good ideas need capital to grow into big companies. From 1996 and until 2003, Doug helped raise more than $100 million from investors to turn his second-bedroom idea into a household name.

In 1996 while in the M.B.A. program, Doug wrote a business plan to raise $650,000 in exchange for thirty percent of Lewisburg Ventures, Inc. Lewisburg Ventures would use the funds primarily to build a web application and market CreditSource via the Internet for two years until it reached positive cash flow. His business plan got second place in a competition at U.Va.

Doug didn't keep his good idea a secret. Instead, he leveraged the law of averages—meaning, the more people he talked to, the better his chances of getting funding. "I was networking with everybody. And maybe I was naïve, but I didn't worry too much about people knocking off the idea," Doug said.

In the beginning he couldn't find anyone interested in investing $650,000, but he found someone willing to consider putting up $10,000. Lee Idleman served on the Board of Trustees at Bucknell and agreed to hear Doug's pitch. "Mr. Idleman," Doug asked, "What would you need to see in order to write a $10,000 check to invest in CreditSource USA?"

Lee gave Doug a straight answer. "Well, Doug, I'd need to see three things: that customers are going to do this; that a bank is going to sign up; and that you have a banker on board who's willing to work for your company. Because I don't know anything about banking, and you don't know anything about banking."

Doug set out to meet Lee's list. First, to prove he could attract customers, probably his toughest obstacle. To find customers, however, Doug faced a typical entrepreneurial quandary: "Which comes first—the chicken or the egg?"

Doug's chicken or egg was that he couldn't get any consumers to apply for loans because he had no banks to book loans. He couldn't get any banks to book loans because he didn't have any consumers "in line" for the banks. "The big question with the banks was: Are consumers really going to do this?" Doug recalls. "The banks asked, 'Why would a consumer put their confidential information on the Internet to fill out a loan application? It's never going to work. Nobody's going to do that.'"

He'd have to *prove* to the banks that consumers would indeed submit a loan request online— otherwise he was stuck. Doug dived into this quandary because he had to start somewhere to overcome his chicken-or-egg dilemma. He designed a marketing test to attract consumers to complete loan applications, even without any banks to fund their requests.

The first step for his faux marketing campaign was to build CreditSource USA a website. Jamey's brother built a basic one at no charge. To attract consumers to the site, Doug invested $1,500 of his own money to buy search-engine keyword advertising from Yahoo, at the time relatively inexpensive.

The campaign attracted more than three hundred borrowers—a stellar result. This marketing test, simple as it was, became a hardy sprout to grow Doug's acorn into a LendingTree. The proof was in the pudding. It turned out that early adopters were easy to find on the Internet and unafraid to apply for a mortgage. Doug had met Lee's first requirement: "Are customers willing to do this?" Check.

The second requirement was to sign a bank. Doug accomplished that—sort of. National City Bank offered him a letter of intent, not quite a full-fledged contract. But Idleman considered its commitment "close enough" because it showed that National City Bank thought CreditSource USA was a viable idea.

Lee's last requirement was for Doug to get a banker to join his team. He didn't quite get an employee, but he did get a former investment banker from Goldman Sachs to join in raising capital. "Well, that's not the kind of banker I was thinking about, but...I guess that'll do," Idleman said. He sent Doug a check for ten thousand dollars. CreditSource USA now had its first investor.

Lee's investment helped Doug obtain other investments to build the first application that would enable banks and borrowers to trade information. The original business plan presumed from discussions with a consultant that building the website and software to run it would be simple. Jamey would be technology adviser, two computer programmers would be paid $15-20 each per hour, and a webmaster would get paid $40,000. Pretty straightforward.

But when they tried to outsource getting the website application built through a small technology consultancy, it didn't work. "My business plan estimates were based on the consultancy that said it would take sixteen weeks. But that team just didn't have a clue."

Doug was now eighteen months and more than a thousand hours into his online mortgage idea, yet he still didn't have a workable product.

"If Don's In, I'm In" (1997)

In June 1997 Doug dropped out of business grad school to commit full-time to CreditSource USA, knowing he'd have to raise more money to get the application built. Doug was also gaining an appreciation for *doing*, not *talking* about doing. "M.B.A.'s are very skeptical, verbal people," Doug says. "A lot of it is Monday morning quarterbacking. Some 25-year-old kid says, 'Clearly what's wrong with Wal-Mart's marketing strategy is...,' he laughs.

Doug wanted to be a doer, not an analyzer of what other people do. Seeing the distinction between doing and talking, and then making the choice to do was an important moment of his entrepreneurial growth. Doug was now all in.

To get the sophisticated technology built, they'd need capital—and lots of it. Doug sent his business plan to Jim Tozer, who had co-founded several banks. Jim had connections with experienced investors like the CEO of marketing giant Young & Rubicon and the former CTO at AOL. "Tozer knew real players," Doug said.

Jim was surprised by Doug's quality business plan and saw

CreditSource USA as a great idea on paper. "I was acquainted with a fellow who was a consummate promoter. He sent me a business plan for what was then called CreditSource and said, 'Jim, read this.' I read it on a plane and I realized that this was a disruptive, transformational idea.

"I thought, 'Oh, my God. This thing really could be something.'"

Raising capital can be like promoting a high school party. A popular kid says to another popular kid, "If you go, I'll go." From these two, the idea of the party gains momentum, and pretty soon you have a real bash on your hands. LendingTree's first big financing went down like that.

First, Doug had to convince the popular kid, Jim Tozer, that he knew what he was doing, so he visited with him in New York. Jim remembers the meeting.

"I had Doug come up and we were sitting around this conference table with two women who'd invested with me before," Jim said. "Doug came in and sang the song, and I said, 'My heavens, I think this guy can actually manage.' Because, you know, there are a zillion good ideas, but the guy with the idea often can't make it move. Doug's package was together. He presented well. He seemed like the kind of person that could manage and sell." One leader can rarely both manage and sell effectively.

Jim considered making a portion of the investment himself, and would help underwrite the rest. But first, he wanted other opinions. He contacted his friend Dick Field to get his perspective. Having just retired from managing a division of the Bank of New York, Dick now was Chairman of Mastercard and had banking experience.

Jim thought, "If Dick's in, I'm in."

Dick liked the deal, but wanted to run it by his friends as well. He especially respected the opinion of Don Colby, who had run credit-card operations for the Bank of New York. Dick told Jim, "If Don's in, I'm in.'

Don Colby became the lynchpin. He set up golf with Doug to learn more about CreditSource USA and the deal itself. As Doug recalls:

"I'm golfing with Don Colby, playing lousy, knowing that this little five-foot Joe Pesci look-alike, a crazy man, was the key to the deal.

"Colby had torn through the business plan and drilled me with questions. I was nervous as hell. I got a twelve on the first hole; just kept hitting it back and forth over the green.

"Probably ten holes in, he said, 'You know, I really like this. I'll put fifty thousand bucks into this thing.' But the fifty thousand wasn't the point—the point was that if he was putting in fifty, Field was putting in two-fifty; Tozer opened the door to the rest of it.

"So Colby was the key. You find these things tend to move in packs. The key is to generate competitive tension because everybody wants to fund what somebody else wants to fund, and nobody wants to fund it if nobody likes it. So the more interest you generate, the easier it is to get ultimate funding."

The investment group headed by Tozer committed to investing one million dollars. But right before closing the deal, Doug received a devastating letter. Morgan Stanley claimed its trademark on "CreditSource." Doug was irate. "I had done some chicken-shit, $50 trademark review to save money. Now I can't use my name. If that letter had come tomorrow, everything would have been OK—at least the money would have been in the bank.

"I stared at myself in the mirror and said, 'Well, let's call them.' I called Tozer and Field and they ripped into me, screaming and yelling 'How did you not know this?'"

Serendipitously, the trademark mistake turned out to be a lucky move, because it forced Doug to find a better name. And now, since they had closed the financing and had money in the bank, they could hire a marketing firm to help them find a more appealing name. When surveying likely customers about a few name choices, the respondents rejected LendingTree. "What the heck is a LendingTree?" they asked. But Doug adopted the name anyway based on additional feedback that reported LendingTree sounded friendly and approachable—which respondents desired in a loan experience.

Doug's idea now had a million dollars and a new name. What steps would he take next?

If I Had a Million Dollars

In a 1993 song, "If I Had a Million Dollars," the Barenaked Ladies surmise that if they had a million dollars, they'd buy a fur coat (with fake fur), a house, a monkey, and other oddities.[12] What would Doug do with a million dollars?

By meeting with dozens of banks, Doug learned their requirements for adopting a tool like LendingTree. Doug would have to build forms to capture data; run filters that allowed banks to input desired loan criteria; and create credit interfaces, file transfer protocols, and login credentials. Consumers needed to be able to log in and view offers, accept or reject offers, and more. The great number of variables required advanced programming.

To make this application work, they'd have to hire someone with advanced programming experience. Since Doug had few personal connections in technology, he just started spreading the word. He stumbled upon technology guru Rick Stiegler through a second-degree connection who attended exercise classes with Rick's wife. Rick was vice president of Advanced Technology at Greenwich Capital Markets and before that had been a high-level technology leader at Morgan Stanley.

Doug believed Rick had what it took, so he offered him a $50,000 salary plus a "boatload of stock," but Rick didn't consider it seriously: "Doug, fifty grand a year wouldn't heat my pool," he said.

But a few months later, LendingTree had raised a million dollars and could now afford to make Rick a serious offer—that he accepted.

They invested more than $300,000 into hiring Rick and hundreds of thousands more in hiring him a technology staff. Without any guarantees that banks would partner with LendingTree, Rick and his team spent several months building a workable application. "We had seven or eight tech guys in there just banging away to build a real application," Doug said.

Investing such a big portion of the first million dollars into technology showed Doug's adaptability as a manager, and his ability to take calculated risks, then live with them. He strategized that superior technology would be a key in selling to future investors. Instead of rushing to market with cheap technology and spending the first million he'd raised on marketing and advertising, he took a more patient, forward-thinking approach, building a solid product first.

A Motley Crew of Investors Determine Doug's Fate (1998)

By early 1998, Rick and his team had done their job. LendingTree had a marketable product with effective technology, but it needed financing to ramp up national marketing and advertising, as well as salespeople who could convince lenders to partner with them.

Doug was again pitching LendingTree to investors. His argument for investing was based upon a mathematical model demonstrating that if you spend a given amount on marketing and advertising, you will attract a predictable number of leads; a set percentage of those leads will convert into closed loans.

The pitch seemed reasonable, except that it made two iffy assumptions: one, the predicted cost to generate each lead, and two, the number of those leads that would result in closed loans. Converting the two assumptions into presumptions would make or break LendingTree.

For several months, Doug traversed the country pitching LendingTree to top-grade investors. He advanced conversations with a few notable firms, but nothing came of his efforts. For example, Intuit, maker of Quicken Mortgage, declined a deal in the eleventh hour. Doug and Jamey flew all the way to California— just to get the ax. "We go walking into the conference room at ten o'clock in the morning, and their head of corporate development comes in and says, 'Guys, I have some bad news. We just had our management meeting and our CEO said we're only allowed to do three investments. And you guys are number four, so we're going to have to just call this off.'"

They got to the last step with Softbank Ventures, a Japanese V.C. that had invested in Yahoo!, but that deal also vaporized.

"We're pitching constantly, and we're getting no, no, no, no...," Doug said of that frustrating period.

But in the spring of 1998 Phoenix Insurance Group invested $3 million because it could leverage LendingTree's technology to reach more customers. The jolt of fresh capital helped Lending-Tree hire up to twenty employees.

By now, two years since its inception, it had raised more than four million dollars but had generated $17,000 in revenue. LendingTree was still just a good idea, though it did have working technology.

Late in 1998, LendingTree raised $7.5 million more from pension fund ULLICO, the Union Labor Life Insurance Company. ULLICO had made its investment based upon a financial forecast, but LendingTree missed those numbers. Fourth quarter 1998 revenue was only $116,000, compared to third quarter's revenue of $100,000—well below the Board's expectations. "We were banking on a huge Q4," Doug said. "So Bob Kennedy at ULLICO basically said, 'Your numbers aren't going to cut it.'"

LendingTree missed its forecast because, first, banks weren't converting leads to closed mortgages to the degree predicted by Doug's mathematical model. Second, the cost of buying keywords from Yahoo! and other search engines had increased due to more competition entering the Internet. Third, an improved website launch was delayed. And fourth, spending more on advertising didn't equate as forecast to a higher proportion of leads. For example, when they spent $1,500, they got 300 leads, but when they spent $150,000 they didn't get 30,000 leads, they got many fewer.

Because Doug had raised money from so many different sources, he realized his partners, who now controlled the board of directors, didn't know him. "I basically had assembled a motley crew of investors. It was scary because the board members didn't actually know me. I was brand new to them. I was a 28-year-old kid. So, it would have been very easy for them to get somebody with more experience and refuse to back me."

Doug was distraught after the board meeting when realizing he might be fired from his company. He and Tara had committed their lives to LendingTree, yet now it might swallow them up. "Look, LendingTree was almost my whole life, and it was Tara's whole life," Doug said. "I mean, we had no personal life balance with our work life. Our lives were truly just work. We used to joke that we couldn't go to dinner without talking about work. Our lives were up early, work late."

Doug thought he was close to losing his idea, his company,

and his work life. But by this time he was practiced in standing up despite turmoil and rejection, so the struggle brought out even more strong qualities. He had learned to turn his fear into fight, pursuing a transparent, team-focused atmosphere with the board by scheduling weekly meetings to update them.

"After the January board meeting when I thought I was going to be fired, I quickly went from being scared to being completely determined to prove myself," Doug says. "I wanted to be totally transparent with the board. I wanted them to believe in the business the way I did. I didn't want to hide anything or be defensive. Also, I needed their advice and buy-in. I knew I needed to be completely candid with them. I needed them to be able to trust me."

During this time, board member and investor Jim Tozer supported Doug and helped him along. "I think everybody needs a mentor who can guide them and get things done. For me, that was Jim." Doug explains. "Especially when things weren't going well."

Tozer remembers spending time with Doug—helping him manage conflict with the board members. "We'd have breakfast when he was in New York," Tozer recalled. "And there was plenty of phone time. I endeavored to see that he stayed focused."

After the January board meeting, the board didn't immediately make a decision as to whether to keep Doug as CEO or fire him. During the first half of 1999, the board had put Doug "on watch." To keep the baby Doug had raised since its inception, he would have to prove himself during the first half of the year.

Scrambling for Revenue (Late 1998 and 1999)

Banks' inability to close leads was hurting LendingTree. They paid LendingTree $300 to $700 when they closed a loan referred by LendingTree, but only $20 for the lead itself before it closed. The banks were buying leads, but they weren't closing them, leaving LendingTree in a hole because the $20 lead fees weren't paying the bills. They needed closed loan fees as well.

LendingTree was burning cash and needed to figure out how to earn near-term revenue. It began private-label licensing its technology to banks, calling it LendX, to run their own online mortgage businesses. LendingTree struck LendX deals with banks like Wachovia and Priceline.com, earning hundreds of thousands in revenue.

Nonetheless, LendingTree's prime business idea was using its website to refer loans. In late 1998 and early 1999, LendingTree finally ramped up that business model from an unexpected source—*mortgage brokers, not banks.* Doug's original business plan had identified mortgage brokers as the competition, not as the group who'd prove that his business idea would work.

As it turned out, mortgage brokers were hungry for leads and LendingTree had them. Doug's business plan had noted that mortgage brokers couldn't compete on price; they could afford to pay a fee to LendingTree and still make money. In this new plan, two levels of brokers assisted in the transaction.

Better yet, the mortgage brokers were entrepreneurial, innovative, receptive to new ideas, and great salespersons; therefore, unlike bankers they could close leads. "The companies that really made LendingTree go were entrepreneurial mom-and-pop mortgage shops—like two guys in their garage who had formed a brokerage in Irvine, California, who said, 'Hey, we'll give these leads a try,'" Doug recalls.

Revenues from mortgage brokers and LendX were helping buy time, but fixing banks' inability to convert their leads to closed loans was a priority for Doug. Clearly, the biggest opportunity was still ahead—referring loans to banks. In 1999 banks and credit unions funded $10.5 trillion in loans compared to $2.8 trillion funded by mortgage brokers and lenders.

In 1999, LendingTree showed progress in improving lead conversion rates. Doug was now winning board approval by correcting the problems that led to LendingTree missing its fourth-quarter 1998 forecast.

LendingTree Hits its Stride (Late 1999 and 2000)

To improve LendingTree's lead-conversion rates with banks, it spent a great deal of time, money, and energy helping the banks close loans referred by LendingTree. That education project to improve bank closure rates worked. In 1999 its number of bank-closed loans increased from a few hundred in January to nearly 3,500 in August. LendingTree facilitated almost a billion in loans that year, helping monthly revenues grow from $200,000 in January to more than $800,000 by August. By late 1999 and early 2000, LendingTree was hitting its growth inflection point.

"The commitment to making money only when the bank made money was probably what made us successful, because it got us in total alignment with our customers. It was my best discovery, and everything was an offshoot of that commitment. Our best practices project led to our understanding of that necessity. If the bank made money, we made money—and only if.

"Whereas our competitors were less focused on customers. And many of those companies didn't make it. To this day, LendingTree actually stands for something unique. We wanted the lenders to be able to build businesses through us."

By November 1999 LendingTree had increased the number of banks in its network to ninety from fewer than twenty a year earlier. It signed big names like Bank One, Bank of America Consumer Finance, Citibank, First USA, and Chase Bank.

The newfound success helped LendingTree attract more investors. On September 20, 1999, LendingTree closed a $50 million financing by selling convertible preferred stock to a group of investors including Capital Z, GE Capital, Goldman Sachs, Marsh and McLennan Risk Capital, priceline.com, and others. "We went out targeting twenty million and ended up raising fifty," Doug says. "As long as we can raise money, we said, 'Let's keep trying to go big. If we had failed to raise the capital, we would have retrenched."

In 1999 and 2000, LendingTree spent much of that money on marketing and advertising, $18.5 million and $56.6 million, respectively. The goal was to obtain high-quality leads for banks— namely consumers with documented income who provide truthful loan applications and have good credit. Doug's strategy for attracting quality leads was advertising in high-quality media— prime-time cable television and radio, for example.

Doug and his marketing team took a risk, hiring a small, creative entrepreneurial advertising agency, Mullen, located "in the woods" near the north shore of Boston.

Mullen created a message for LendingTree based upon "empathy for the consumer." The goal was to empower the customer, letting them know that they could analyze the field of competition and simply and easily make the best choice. Mullen suggested using friendly humor and customers' well-documented frustration with the mortgage process as the tone for the advertising by including the tagline, "When banks compete, you win." The goal for the first campaign was to establish brand and educate the market.

LendingTree's first television commercial, "Rejection," featured a casually-dressed couple in their middle-class kitchen interviewing bankers in three-piece suits.

The couple speaks to two bankers at their kitchen table: "Your rates are a little high. What's the word I'm thinking of? ... NO!" [couple laughs.]

The couple repeats "NO!" to several bankers, each time laughing at them in a mocking tone. One scene features the husband eating ice cream next to his open refrigerator while laughing at a disappointed banker.

The television commercials worked well. Doug attributes much of LendingTree's success to paying for marketing that drove high-quality leads for banks. "Our marketing drove real customers into the process. The whole company was focused on finding and passing along high-quality leads." Every phase of the marketing project had to be effective, not wasting anyone's time, effort, and/ or money.

And the Rest is History

In February 2000, LendingTree completed a public offering by selling twenty-one percent of its stock for $43.8 million. The transaction's valuation was $207 million— impressive considering that its 1999 revenue was $7 million! But during that time, capital was pouring into technology and online businesses, so LendingTree benefitted from the trend.

During the tech bubble, critics labeled LendingTree a struggling internet company. In Doug's office hangs a blown-up 2001 *Fortune Magazine* feature entitled, "Collapse of the E-Universe."[13] The graphic is a black solar system with E-companies - represented by planets, all rocketing towards the sun. The thesis of the piece is that the E-companies closest to the sun will "burn up" and run out of cash first. The E-company second-closest to the sun? LendingTree. "We were nowhere close to running out of cash," Doug says. "They just didn't understand our balance sheet and how we make money."

LendingTree proved the pundits wrong and its revenue grew to $30.8 million in 2000, $64 million in 2001, and $111.4 million in 2002. In 2002 it funded 285,000 loans worth $21.9 billion, helping it earn a profit of $8.9 million even after spending $50.1 million on advertising and marketing.

In August 2003, IAC/Interactive, a $6.3 billion revenue media empire, acquired LendingTree for $726 million ($21.67 per share) through a stock-swap transaction. Soon after, Doug was promoted to president of IAC/Interactive. In 2006 LendingTree's revenue increased to $476 million, but after the residential real-estate market crashed in September 2008, the company struggled in meeting further growth expectations.

In August 2008, IAC/Interactive spun off LendingTree into a separate publicly-traded company, Tree.com, and Doug became its Chairman and CEO. Since the spinoff, Tree has diversified its revenues and generated helpful new products, including GetSmart. com (loans for insurance and college), RealEstate.com, Degree-Tree.com, HealthTree.com, LendingTreeAutos.com, DoneRight. com, and InsuranceTree.com.

Conclusion
In which a forest from little acorns grows.

In January 1994 Stanford Ph.D. graduate students Jerry Yang and David Filo were supposed to be doing dissertation research on how to make computer chips run faster. Instead they became fixated on their hobby—the World Wide Web. Frustrated by an inability to organize their favorite websites online, they built a software program to sort websites into subject-matter categories.

Their good idea would become Internet giant Yahoo!

Yang and Filo used the software to create a website that organized and published their favorite sites, calling it "Jerry and David's Guide to the World Wide Web." Soon they were spending more time on their website than on their dissertation.

"We eventually spent more hours cataloguing web links than we did working on our thesis," Yang told said in his 2009 commencement speech at the University of Hawaii. "We slept on the floor of our trailer—one of us would be programming and dealing with our little [Web]site, and the other would sleep. We did it out of love and passion. We never thought it would turn into a business, we just figured that if people kept coming to our site, we were doing a great service and ... having fun!"[14]

The website's popularity grew fast, and after several months they changed its name to "Yahoo" because they liked its meaning: "a rude, unsophisticated, uncouth person." And seeing its growing popularity, Yang and Filo came to a vision for Yahoo!: to become an amazing consumer interface that would outlive them—not just a search engine whose primary purpose was to earn money.

By 1995 Yahoo!'s website became so popular that the servers at Stanford were overloaded, so the administration requested that Yahoo! find a new home. In order to pay for the servers and website administration, they sought advice from five venture capital funds, and Sequoia Capital invested $2 million in their idea.

Sequoia helped Yang and Filo consider growth strategies.They decided to recruit a CEO with business experience to help them fulfill their vision for Yahoo!, fellow Stanford graduate Tim Koogle, who ran a $400-million company, Intermec, to become Yahoo!'s CEO and only its sixth employee. Koogle helped Yahoo! develop an online advertising revenue model, which in 1996 was a new concept. Yang and Filo became "Chief Yahoos" and helped advance technology and promote Yahoo!

Yang says that at the time he didn't want to be his company's CEO. "People always ask me why I took myself out of the day-today operating responsibility," Yang says. "But that's never what I wanted to do, and besides, I knew so little about business that I didn't want to slow things down when the company began to scale up."[15]

Mike Moritz, a director at Sequoia Capital, says that Jerry isn't an entrepreneur trying to make a quick buck and bring attention to himself, but instead he wants Yahoo to endure like a mighty oak tree: "Jerry would be considered an unusual entrepreneur today because he actually wanted to build a lasting company. He's not... another grotesque Doonesbury caricature of an entrepreneur."[16]

Koogle's management skills buoyed Yahoo!'s early growth from a good idea in a graduate-school trailer into a growth-company business. Koogle established distribution and technology alliances in order to compete with other search engines also backed with capital, such as Alta Vista, Lycos, and Infoseek. And in April 1996 he helped Yahoo! raise $33 million in a public stock offering.

In September 2012, Yahoo had more than 14,000 employees and a market capitalization of more than $18.5 billion dollars.

Great management is the impetus for creating large, high-growth innovative businesses. Fast-growing companies need experienced leaders to manage the complexity that comes along with growth: hiring and managing qualified employees; selling and marketing products; processing and fulfilling customer orders; providing customer service; maintaining and upgrading products and technology; reporting and controlling finances; and developing strategies to ensure investor returns.

The paradox for many innovative entrepreneurs is that the independent, creative mindset desirable during any start-up phase gets them to a certain point, but if they decide to grow, they must morph into a business-oriented, operational, strategic mindset. This necessary transition is as hard to accomplish as an emotional and cognitive transformation. An entrepreneur's inability to change his or her mindset is often why good ideas remain small or fail. The leader refuses to let go of a creation-mode mentality and that inability to adapt holds his creation back. Such a leader doesn't hire the best, or fire the worst as he should; instead he maintains control at best, and keeps life easy, predictable, and stress-free.

Doug Lebda is a rare blend of a creative, risk-taking starter and a strategic-minded executive who adapted to and fostered scalable growth. In his second bedroom, he created the idea to broker loans online, figured out how his idea could work, and took financial and personal risks to turn his idea into reality. In the beginning, he was a creative, independent, risk-taking entrepreneur. For example, even before he had a product, he cold-called banks with nothing in hand except a brochure. And he invested $1,500 when he had little money to run a marketing test that proved his idea could work. He and his wife, Tara, worked tirelessly and with limited resources from their second bedroom. During the start-up phase, Doug was the consummate bootstrapping, trial-and-error entrepreneur.

But once LendingTree took root, Doug switched from being an innovative, survival-minded entrepreneur into a cool-headed corporate-minded executive. He learned to take responsibility and balance the disparate interests of a wide range of stakeholders: customers, banks, partners, investors, and employees. Jim Tozer says that Doug was a leader who figured out how to lead a large company.

"Doug was quite a good strategist. And as smart as he was, he still communicated with a lot of people. So he didn't go dream ideas up himself. He'd talk to enough people and learned from them and incorporated what they told him to do. He was good in that way.

"And Doug marshaled talented people well. When his friends

were not good enough for the job, he replaced them. He did not stick with losers for very long. And Doug managed to do it in ways that kind of worked. I mean no one really threw hand grenades back. So Doug built a good team and he reassigned people in the right kind of way in his team so the right thing was being done along the way."

In addition to Jim's perceptions, Doug's management skills were evident throughout his building of LendingTree, and those skills opened up opportunities for him:

His convincingly written business plan and presentation skills attracted well-heeled investors like Jim Tozer. "My heavens, I think this guy can actually manage," Tozer said the first time he met him.

He recruited world-class experts in various fields, like Rick Stiegler, who built LendingTree's technology.

He handled the pressure when LendingTree's directors grilled Doug for missing a quarterly goal. He was executive-like, thoughtful, and strategic—not selfish or defensive. He didn't run or escape in place, but he strategized to improve revenues, meeting weekly with directors to seek their input and improve the business.

On the way to his original goal, Doug was flexible, morphing LendingTree's business model by licensing his technology (LendX) and encouraging business from mortgage brokers until he figured how to help banks close LendingTree's referred loans.

Barry Diller recognized Doug's management skills, and after IDC acquired LendingTree, he promoted Doug to president of IAC.

From 10,000 acorns, only one oak tree grows to maturity. But Ralph Waldo Emerson points out the potential if conditions are favorable: "The creation of a thousand forests is in one acorn."[17] One small acorn can produce a tree that produces thousands of acorns every year. From there, more trees can grow, and soon a forest.

That's how capitalism works, too. An innovator can do anything he or she pleases with a good idea. He can allow it to go to waste, keep it small so that it produces just a little fruit, or he can focus, grow it into a large, successful company like LendingTree or Yahoo!. These growth businesses make our economy go. George Gilder, author of *The Spirit of Enterprise* (1985), writes, "Society is always in deep debt to the entrepreneurs who sustain it and [who] rarely consume by themselves more than the smallest share of what they give society."[18]

Doug is one of those entrepreneurs to whom Gilder refers. Doug Lebda has created thousands of jobs and hundreds of millions of dollars in new wealth that has been put to work in other innovative ways. Doug has built an American forest.

But to build a big, innovative company, lots of investment capital is required, and therefore, great management skills are required to see a goal, gather relevant facts, make a persuasive case, and encourage and convince the right investors to come aboard and help build the best team for that project. If the founder doesn't have those skills, the experience, or a desire to manage, then releasing his or her control and allowing someone else to take the reins is paramount.

Sometimes getting the right manager to nurture a giant oak requires that the founder step aside and recruit an experienced business person to become CEO, as did Jerry Yang and David Filo. Or sometimes, if he or she is up for/to the difficult challenge, the founder can remain CEO, like Doug did.

But either way, the key is being willing and able to cede control to others when business reasons call for that decision. LendingTree grew into a mighty oak because Doug *facilitated* its success, instead of controlling it.

Chapter 3
Brian Hamilton's Sageworks:
Summoning the Grit To Keep On

Not every start-up's growth curve looks exactly like a hockey stick. For example, Sageworks' curve is a "delayed" hockey stick. In the beginning, its revenue growth was tracking to look like a hockey stick when during its third year revenue started growing. Then something unusual occurred—revenue flat-
tened out again for three more years, delaying growth.

Sageworks figured out a new plan and hit a second growth inflection point—and this one took off— thanks partly to CEO and founder Brian Hamilton's grit, a huge help to innovative entrepreneurs.

Introduction

Sageworks is a fast-growing financial information company whose flagship product, *ProfitCents,* helps hundreds of thousands of small business owners gain an understanding of their financial statements. Its value proposition argues that small business owners are often inexperienced with balance sheets, income statements, and financial ratios, thus not able to use that information effectively to improve their business or to save it from foundering.

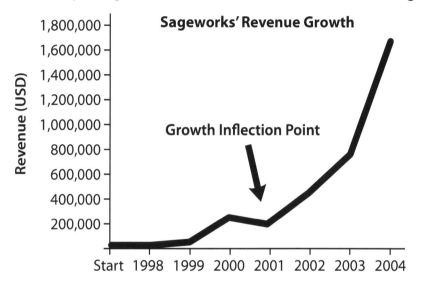

ProfitCents to the rescue!

Here's how *ProfitCents* works. The owner of a printing company (or his CPA) inserts his tax return's financial data into *ProfitCents*, and the program automatically generates a three-to-five-page report of financial advice in plain English. An excerpt from a report says, "In 2009 XYZ Printing Company's net profitability reduced at a faster rate than debt, which is not a favorable result in the short run."

Sageworks doesn't publish its revenue, but in 2016 it is still growing fast and has hundreds of employees. Sageworks is regularly cited in business magazines such as *Forbes* and *Businessweek*, and Brian is regularly interviewed on CNBC.

Today Sageworks' Brian Hamilton is in his suburban Raleigh, N.C., office conference room with teammates, drawing football plays on a whiteboard to illustrate product strategy. He's six feet tall with a medium build, light, sandy-blond hair, and blue eyes. Dressed in blue jeans, a light blue button-down Oxford shirt, white ankle golf socks, and brown shoes, Brian looks as though he woke up late on a Saturday, ran off to a quick breakfast, then to the office. Not a CEO to stand on ceremony, it is clear the man is here to work.

ProfitCents' success has led to Sageworks' creation of a plethora of related financial software solutions. But when Brian Hamilton first started Sageworks, it wasn't the slam-dunk idea it is today. Nothing about it was obvious or necessary. Building *ProfitCents* was a daunting task, making Sageworks' idea-to-reality story a near-perfect slog up a mountain of entrepreneurial grit.

The source of entrepreneurial grit is determination—long-term perseverance and the founder's passion to achieve a goal. The gritty innovator presses on, often over several years, despite hardship, disappointment, and boredom. And just when it seems logical to cut his losses, he stays the course—clawing away day in and day out, year after year.

And think of grit's alternative meaning: hard, coarse-grained sandstone used in making grindstones to wear down rough edges. Grind that meaning with stubborn courage, brave perseverance, and heart, and that's Brian, a man of content over style, and action over talk.

Just Shoot Me Now

At eight, Brian was already an entrepreneur in his Connecticut neighborhood. "I was the guy cutting lawns, doing rough sealant... that was my life." But despite his being a self-starter, he didn't excel as a high school student and had a G.P.A. of 1.6. "I barely got out of the place," he laments.

Instead of pursuing academics, Brian ran out onto the football field. He credits football's culture of setting and attaining personal goals with teaching him lessons that later helped him create and build Sageworks.

From 1981 to 1985 Brian attended Sacred Heart University in Connecticut, a place Brian admits had few admission standards. The first in his family to attend college, he took advantage of his time there by earning good grades and becoming president of the student government.

After graduating, he worked for a bank in Connecticut. The experience grated on his independent nature—but nurtured his entrepreneurial desires. Brian didn't like being managed. "I worked for a woman named Rose in the bank's credit department and she was all over me. I'm never going to be in a micromanaged environment again—working from 8:30 to 4:45. I don't know how to explain her management style. Like, she'd demand I change 'that' into 'those.' The pointless nitpicking ruined my confidence."

"There's something in the human spirit that really calls out for people to have clarity on win and lose. I want to know, 'Did I do a good job?' I paint my porch, then I get something done. But when I worked at the bank, I never felt like I was accomplishing anything. And, that's frustrating and, you know, it's so American, too. We want to know—win? lose? We want clarity, man. In a world that's really unclear, you want clarity and a continuation of that aspect of sports. Boy, you sure get it with entrepreneurship."

In a way, Rose "helped" Brian into his entrepreneurial prowl. After only one year at the bank, he applied to graduate schools. Because of his good collegiate grades, high test scores, and banking experience, in 1988 he was accepted into Duke University's M.B.A. program. Like that of the bank, though, Duke M.B.A.'s big-business mentality further brought out his defiance of rigid structure and control.

"At Duke, walking those antiseptic, beautiful halls, I thought,

'Okay, I know I don't want this. I don't want a career in corporate America. Shoot me now if I have to work for an investment bank or a consulting firm or a big corporation.' At that point, prison would have been better. 'Alright—prison or IBM? I'll take prison. I just won't work for IBM!'"

Understanding his own need to be in control helped Brian plan his career. At Duke, he learned what he wanted to do after he graduated: start businesses. But for the first two years after graduating, Brian didn't know what type of business to start, so he meandered. "I was kind of be-bopping around, frankly," Brian recalls. "I did some small real estate projects in a 'non-career' career. All I knew is what I *didn't* want to do. I didn't ever want to be back in a position like I was in at the bank again, to be honest."

In 1993 Brian owned a Laundromat and grew it into a small chain. That experience helped him learn from his mistakes. "I was doing everything the wrong way…pursuing the wrong financing, hiring the wrong people. Those years were a training period.

"And then, of course, I started Sageworks."

Phase I: Sageworks' Conception (1993 – 1998)

In 1993, while teaching a continuing-ed finance class at Duke, Brian made a quick calculation on the board, speculating that, "If this small business could receive payment from its customers in 30 days instead of 40, it could earn $20,000 more in profit each year.

"You know," he told the class, "it's amazing someone hasn't automated this."

A student, Sarah Tourville, a 25-year veteran software developer at Unisys, approached Brian in the hallway after class. "If you can develop that system, I can program it."

"I was just sorta like, 'Whatever,'" Brian said, considering his idea a throwaway.

Brian and Sarah stayed in touch, though. Four years came and went, with Brian occasionally thinking about the idea. In 1997, he got serious. "I knew from my banking experience and from being a business owner, that people needed something like this," Brian says. "I thought, 'Maybe I should give this a shot.'"

The timing was good for Brian to start an innovative business. He had recently sold some real estate and two Laundromats, so he had some cash. He felt like he was at the right age—thirty-five. He also simply "just wanted to do it."

But his decision to start Sageworks wasn't a one-time epiphany. Instead it "morphed," as he recalls. "Funny how things start. They usually start slowly. You like to think you have some grand vision, but usually you just start groping along and then it develops energy."

Brian started Sageworks with low expectations. "I knew the odds were against me. Starting Sageworks was my long pass. It's third down and 15 and I'm throwing the ball long. I don't expect anyone to catch it. 'We'll give it a try and see what happens.' That's what I figured."

The name Sageworks came from Brian's desire to find a word that denoted wisdom, and he liked the word, "Sage." One night while watching a movie, "Dreamworks" came across the screen and the name hit him, "Wow…Sageworks!"

Brian invested about $200,000 to start Sageworks. He needed money for personal living expenses, a few employees, filing a patent, and paying rent and other overhead. He wasn't worried about losing the money. "I didn't care. You have to be somewhat that way. At some point there has to be that ingredient that if it fails, it fails." Brian felt he could always make money somehow—so he rolled the dice, betting financially on his new venture.

Brian's nothing-to-lose approach isn't uncommon among entrepreneurs. One of Virgin's founder and CEO, Richard Branson's, favorite sayings is: "Screw it, let's do it."[19]

Brian Hamilton believes that non-entrepreneurs may not relate as easily to this mindset. "I know a fair number of entrepreneurs who have failed. Non-entrepreneurs ask them, 'Why did you fail?' or 'What did you learn from it?' Those people don't understand entrepreneurship. Entrepreneurs say, 'I tried it and it didn't work. So what? That doesn't define me. I'm just going to try something else.'"

He says the careful, can't-lose type is often not cut out for entrepreneurship because of fear of failure and loss of huge sums of money. "I've seen people succeed to death in their lives. In high school they were captain of their football team, and then they went to college, did great, and got a great job. That guy is never going to start a business because he can't fail. He's never failed at anything." Success is partly a matter of "practicing failure" and seeing that you don't die from it. You pick yourself up and try something else.

Phase II: Product Creation
(January 1998 – June 1999)

To make his product idea work, Brian figured Sageworks needed a software application and the artificial intelligence to produce narrative advice. Brian paid Sarah to develop the software and also gave her ten percent of Sageworks' stock.

Brian set out to write the artificial intelligence. He set up a small office at an incubator where the rent was cheap. He figured writing the artificial intelligence would be simple. "I thought it would take thirty days!" Brian laughs.

But creating the formulas turned out to be as complicated as sorting out a big bowl of wet spaghetti. Each report would require thousands of "section assemblies," something like a series of related algorithms. Creating a system that could automatically generate each individual client's series was like solving a Rubik's cube several thousand times.

Each type of business had to have its special characteristics and "rules" analyzed and written down in the actual order in which they occurred, adding complexity to the problem of finding the most accurate description of the process. A restaurant's financial accounting process looks different from a steel manufacturer's.

In all, the product required 10,000 manually written pages of text. For over a year and half, Brian spent six days a week, ten hours a day "in the zone" writing financial outcomes. In all, he spent at least 5,000 hours of sweat equity creating Sageworks' product.

Brian wrote his formula and 10,000 pages of text, not knowing whether anyone would care about them—much less buy them, often feeling "stupid" and "lonely" during the eighteen months' development. "I thought, 'If I write this song and play it, will anybody actually listen to it?' That feeling of isolation is often the biggest obstacle to starting a business."

But the tedious experience of building Sageworks made him more resilient in the long run. He learned to turn feelings of despair into a hunger for survival. So later on when the chips were down, he'd remember, then press on like he'd done when writing financial outcomes for months on end at the business incubator.

Phase III: Discovering a Market
(1999 – 2002)

By June 1999, the product was ready to sell, but who was most likely to buy it? Small business owners? Banks? And *how* would Sageworks sell its product? Brian wasn't sure, so he went to work trying things.

Brian's business plan outlined several marketing concepts for Sageworks, but years later he considers it a "joke and ill-founded. The financial projections were ridiculous," he says. "It's sort of like, there's 27 million businesses in the country and if we get 1% of them paying us X dollars a month, we'll be at $400 million in three years. You know—one of those things."

Brian branded the product *ProfitCents* to help potential buyers identify with its value: understanding financials. He built a website and marketed online, selling a few reports to individual banks for $14 each. Those small sales were a start, but not much.

Then that fall, while looking for ideas to help this big bank help its small business customers, a manager found Sageworks on a search engine. Two months later, the bank licensed *ProfitCents* for $250,000. Brian was ecstatic. He thought, "Wow, this huge bank licensed our product. There's something here!"

Now Sageworks would take off. The bank was going to leverage his solution, and soon other financial institutions would follow suit. So in 2000 Brian did what most technology companies did then—he raised capital and later regretted it. Sageworks raised $500,000 from investors by selling five to ten percent of the company's stock, mostly to people he knew. From then on, he felt responsible for their money. "It was a totally different dynamic after that," Brian said.

Feeling responsible for other people's money is a more weighty responsibility than being independent, with a "nothing-left-to-lose" approach to business. By raising money, Brian now felt pressure from investors.

And after he had the money, no more banks called. To make matters worse, the bank's use of the product disappointed, not working well for its customers. "It looked and sounded good at first," Brian says. "It was like a shiny-girl; good-looking and everything, but inside there was nothing there." Brian learned the hard way that bankers spend most of their time making loans and selling products, and they have little time for minute financial analysis.

Worse yet, when Sageworks raised capital, it had hired more employees—creating weighty overhead expenses. Since its new employees didn't have an obvious market to sell to, the company was operating in organized chaos. "I don't recall what the heck we were doing," Brian says. "We were working hard with no end point, really."

Between 2000 and 2002 Sageworks wasn't having much sales success. They tried selling to franchises, small businesses, web marketers, Chamber of Commerce offices, but they couldn't get it to go.

The company also faced financial difficulties. In 2000 it had spent about $300,000 but had minimal revenue, so it was running out of money. "You could see the end," Brian said. Nobel prize recipient Ernest Rutherford once said at a similar crisis point, "Gentlemen, we have run out of money. It is time to start thinking."[20]

But Brian didn't overanalyze his predicament – he kept fighting and kept looking for customers. He got in his car and drove across the country making sales calls on anyone who'd visit with him: H&R Block, American Express, Fair Isaac, several banks, and some small financial firms.

Brian's scrappy road trip paid off. A major financial software firm, wanted to strike a deal with Sageworks. The firm was seemingly a good fit because its business mission was like Sageworks'— both wanted to make financial tools easier to use.

The software firm's chief technology officer asked Brian to meet with its co-founder, and grow it to more than a billion in revenue. The conversation felt more like an inquisition than an introductory meeting. The cofounder/executive relentlessly grilled Brian.

"We're trying to make financial analysis easy," Brian opened.

"Why would anybody even want this?" The executive returned.

"Well, it helps them understand their financial statements."

"Why would they want to do that?"

"To help them make better decisions."

"How would it help them to do that?"

"Because they'll understand their cash flow."

Brian felt the executive was trying to make him prove that "White is white" or "Black is black." Frustrated and flustered, after forty-five minutes Brian cordially ended the meeting—convinced he had failed.

The meeting was a defining moment for Brian because the executive's doubt inspired Brian's "I'll-show-you!" fire in the belly.

Despite the disappointing meeting with the executive, Brian soon heard from the software firm. "Brian, we've got some good news," the CIO told him. "We'd like to license your technology."

The software firm paid Sageworks $250,000 per year for the right to publish a free "lite version" *ProfitCents* report for each of its business customers. The software firm's customers could pay to upgrade to a full-version *ProfitCents* report.

But very few did.

The partnership with this software firm didn't work because Sageworks got very few upgrades. Perhaps the executive's doubts had been well founded?

The failed partnership with the software was Sageworks' second big blow. The first had been the big bank's project a year earlier that also went nowhere because a successful interface between the bank and its customers had never been closed. These "false-positives" were crushing blows for Brian. "The hardest part is the feeling of 'Where is this going?' I think that's why most people give up," Brian says. They can't come up with the answer before both their confidence and their money run out.

In 2002, almost two and half years after Brian started marketing *ProfitCents*, he still hadn't discovered a viable market to sell to. But he didn't give up.

Phase IV: Discovering and Developing the CPA Market (2002 - 2004)

When Brian was traveling around the country "looking for wins," he felt a small glimmer of hope when he sold a $500 subscription to a small, regional CPA firm in Knoxville, Tennessee. On a whim, he asked one of his senior managers, Drew White, to explore the CPA market further.

Drew beat the bushes for a few months and made a few more sales to CPA firms. He learned that CPAs already provide the type of advice to small businesses that *ProfitCents* calculates, but most importantly, Drew discovered that *ProfitCents* saves them time. And for CPA firms, as for every business, time is money.

Brian had discovered a viable market—in fact, a large viable market. Manta.com, for example, lists 132,645 accounting companies on its public website.[21] With such a large market, Sageworks could stop grabbing at straws and instead focus on a market where it was confident there was a clear need.

Sageworks needed something to rally around, and selling almost exclusively to CPA firms was it. Brian's employees were tired of shooting in the dark. Now they had a sales and marketing focus.

In 2002 Sageworks turned its cannons on CPA firms. Brian, Drew, and three other experienced salespersons spent most of their day telemarketing to them. Customer acquisition became like a manufacturing process—if they made a hundred calls, they'd talk to four people and get one demo. For every two or three firms that took a demo, one would sign up as a customer. "You could line them up," Brian said, "and predict that one out of three hundred would close."

Sageworks sales-conversion ratio was low partly because it is difficult to educate a market about a new product. To its five salespersons, *ProfitCents'* value proposition was obvious, but the typical CPA had difficulty grasping the concept.

If a salesperson was lucky enough to get a CPA on the phone, he explained how *ProfitCents* puts numbers into narrative form—plain English.

"But why would I want to do that?" the CPA asked.

"Because your client may not understand the financial data you're giving to them."

"I'm not sure they'd want a written report like that," the CPA countered. "What would my customer do with the report? How much time would it take to explain it to them?"

Most firms couldn't, or wouldn't, grasp this basic concept—not because of any lagging intelligence, but because of their ingrained habits. They weren't accustomed to providing such reports to their clients, even if it was a good idea, and they didn't want to start now.

Sageworks' dilemma exemplifies the entrepreneur's difficult task of educating a market about any innovation. Brian illustrates the dilemma with a story about the spoon:

"Let's say it's 1300 in Europe, and an entrepreneur is selling spoons for the first time. He sees a man's got two hands on the bowl and he's holding it to his mouth sipping the soup. The entrepreneur shows him, 'Hey, here's something I invented. I call it a spoon. And you can dip it in the bowl, fill it with soup, and raise the spoon to your mouth.' The entrepreneur sees the value, and thinks the man will say, 'Got it! Gimme!'" He smiles, expecting the man to grab and use the spoon. But he doesn't want the spoon because the marketplace doesn't act that way. The target customer asks, 'What hand do I hold it in? Can I hold it with two hands? Why is it round? When do I use it? Do I use it to eat spaghetti? Why not?'

"And the things that are clear to the entrepreneur might be wrong. The man drinking the soup might be happy to continue doing so if he's in a country that has only tomato soup—he doesn't need a spoon; he can sip it fine. He doesn't have big chunks of chicken or potato to lift out of it.

"And entrepreneurs can be arrogant: 'Well, my idea is a great idea and everyone should use it.' But the man with the bowl of tomato soup says, 'I don't know about that.' The result is unsuccessful interface, and the spoon stays nestled in the entrepreneur's sample case as he tramps from town to town."

Each Sageworks' salesperson sold only about $100,000 worth of subscriptions per year. But most of the CPAs who purchased *ProfitCents* liked it, and paid to renew their software subscription. Thanks in part to the renewals, revenues steadily improved to over $400,000 in 2002, $700,000 in 2003, and over $1,600,000 in 2004.

Between 2002 and 2004, Sageworks was hitting its growth inflection point. Sageworks was on its way, finally transitioning from a good idea into a growing business. But to get there, the growth curve was small. "In 2001, we had maybe fifty clients,"

Brian says. "By 2004 we had like five hundred. Fifty to five hundred sounds like a lot, but if you consider it in terms of revenues—it's still small."

Brian's process of discovering Sageworks' optimal market, CPAs, may appear inefficient. Indeed, more diligent research and planning might have helped him discover it earlier. Today *ProfitCents'* biggest market, CPAs, seems obvious for Sageworks. So why didn't Brian investigate the accounting market *before* he started Sageworks?

The answer lies in shades of gray. Hindsight, especially in the field of innovative entrepreneurship, produces 20/20 vision. Seemingly obvious solutions are often not so obvious when a start-up's in discovery mode. Trial and error, not pure planning, is more likely to reveal market reality. Sure, Brian may have sped up his successful efforts by interviewing several possible markets before he started selling.

But interviews and focus groups don't reveal the same information as a closed sale. The best way to discover a market is by selling to it—not by researching it. Until the sale of a real product is closed, it is difficult to understand completely the viability of a market. What people *say* they like, versus what people *sacrifice* to buy it, are two totally different things. The result is that an entrepreneur rarely learns what customers really want until they start asking for the sale.

Brian credits Sageworks Software-as-a-Service (SaaS) business model to help it grow and become viable. The SaaS model charges its customers an annual fee, similar to how a magazine bills its customers, to access the software and database—instead of traditional software that licensed software for one fee upfront. During the first year selling to CPAs, the average annual fee was about $1,000. Month-to-month, Sageworks' revenue was erratic.

But at the beginning of the second year, the salesman is prospecting for new customers, but—and here's the key point—the first-year customer who's renewed doesn't need a lot of his time to stay satisfied with Sageworks. And, with the exception of updating the financial data, that's almost pure profit—and reliable growth.

"If we were a traditional software company, and we had to start the dial every year from zero," Brian says. "[Without renewals] we never would have made it. Never. Never," Brian recalls. "Because do the math. If you sell a hundred thousand dollars per sales guy, and you're paying [him] sixty or seventy thousand [to find and close the customer] and then you add other sales overhead like rent, travel, and other expenses, you don't make money until you get the renewal."

Phase V: The Underdog Defends Its Turf (2004)

In 2004 Sageworks faced new growth challenges – the first one coming from a much larger potential competitor. The competitor was already selling to CPA firms and approached Sageworks to acquire it, but after brief negotiations, its executives tried to bully Brian; if he didn't sell to them at a favorable price, they would compete with him.

"These guys come in and say, 'We want to buy you.' I say 'Wow, that's terrific.' They take me out for dinner, wine and dine me with cigars and all that stuff. And then the next day, they get me in a room in front of all their executives and, as I interpreted it, basically said, 'You'll either sell to us at a favorable price, or we'll introduce a competitive product and just crush you. I got up, I closed my laptop, and said, 'OK, guys, it was good to meet you. Thanks for the meal.' Walked out.

"We're this tiny little company with 15 employees and maybe 500 customers, if we're lucky. They're a division of a multibillion-dollar company and worth several hundred million dollars. And I'm like, 'You're picking on me!' I mean if you want to learn about my company, that's fine. But don't bully me. They absolutely did that. I'm Irish, so I was like, 'OK, conversation's over. We're at war now. Shields are up. Oh, and you might beat me, by the way, but it's not gonna be easy for you.'"

After the corporate bully's ultimatum, Brian was forced to make a decision— either sell for a low price or compete against a multi-billion-dollar company. Brian first wanted to gauge how serious the competitor was about their threat to compete. He learned more when Drew, shortly after that meeting, attended a trade show with their head of sales, who told him, "We've got forty people developing a competing product to yours."

Brian was concerned that the competitor would develop a cheaper version of his product and "blow them out." But after seeking counsel from his management team, he decided to compete with them instead of selling out. Even so, Brian felt as if he had "two 18-inch cannons pointed at my head."

In response, Sageworks raised $4 million in capital from investors to improve its product quality and gain market share.

"Here's what we did: We started hiring more people because we knew what the competitor's play would be. They would come at us with one product, expecting we'd go head to head. But no. If you're coming out with one product, I'm gonna have three. When you have three, I'm gonna have six. So where we really beat them was on the product side. They have one product and we have like twenty that do different financial-analysis things."

Sageworks won the war against the larger competitor in just that way. After a few years, the larger competitor fizzled out and began giving its product away for free. "So the competitor had been a nuisance, but they haven't been a problem," Brian says.

But as in most wars, practically speaking, there is no winner. Everyone is left wounded and hurt. For example, raising so much capital was a decision Brian regretted because he felt that he overreacted to the threat. "That's where I made a mistake that I wouldn't make again. But I didn't know any better! It was a bad strategic play because I should have known my customers better. They wouldn't buy a chcap substitute. They need a decent product because they're CPA's. So the competitor didn't do any real damage at all, almost none. But in response to a perceived threat, we raised too much cash for our company, and that was damaging."

Brian regrets raising capital because of ownership dilution. But he is fortunate that despite Sageworks' taking another round of funding, Brian still owns a majority of its shares and thus retains control. "It's a simple formula. Keep 51%," Brian advises. "The big argument to me was always, 'Well, I'd rather have 10% of a billion-dollar company, than 100% of a million-dollar company.' But that is typically a very weak argument because the dream gets lost in execution. There are only 200 software companies in the world that do over $100 million in revenue. So figure it out—now, which would you rather have?

"What's real is when you give away control of your company. This friend of mine started with venture capital and sure enough … he lost control of the company and got fired and the VC guys ran the thing into the gutter."

Also in response to the threat from the competitor, Sageworks grew too fast.

"We started scaling the company real quickly. To compete, we weren't trying to get 30%-a-year growth, we were trying to get 500%! And our losses started really escalating because we were trying to grow too fast: We hired too many people, we fired too many people, and we lost money. I would never again over-respond to a competitive threat— even if they are a billion-dollar company."

Telemarketing: Hard-Won Revenue (2004-2008)

In 2004 because of the competitive threat, Sageworks aggressively acquired market share. Its average subscription cost was still about $1,000 per year – too small to visit prospects in person. On the other hand, the average subscription was too large for credit card e-commerce transactions, especially considering that *ProfitCents* was a new idea and e-commerce was in its infancy. CPAs rarely made $1,000 online purchases from companies they'd never heard of. The market would have to be educated before e-commerce was realistic for Sageworks' subscription sales. Sageworks' customer acquisition strategy did include telemarketing, though, and it invested a good portion of its $4 million in fresh capital to hire salespersons to cold-call CPA firms.

While selling came naturally to Brian and his management team, they had little experience managing a telemarketing center. They'd have to make up their strategy as they went along. For example, they figured that they could easily teach young college graduates to sell as capably as they themselves did, but that plan didn't go smoothly:

"We taught the kids the wrong way to sell. Like, 'I'm just going to just give it to you, and force it down your throat.' And that doesn't work. And now I realize why—because they never got the practice. And so we let those people down. I had been selling ever since I was a kid, and I couldn't understand why everyone couldn't sell.

"So, fundamentally, between 2002 and 2008 we made the massive mistake of thinking we could build a big direct-sales force with a lot of capable salespeople, when in fact, we learned the Pareto Principle—that we always had 20% of the people selling 80% of the deals."

The Pareto Principle maintains that production is not evenly distributed. And, often times, when the few produce the most, it's detrimental to workplace harmony. Embracing this principle is a difficult part of growth transition for entrepreneurs because many times the first employees are all productive. These first employees are likely hand-selected, they acquire ownership, and they embrace the new idea. But as a business becomes larger, its growing number of employees becomes less vested, and, therefore, high producers in that number are more difficult to find and train.

By 2006 Sageworks employed 70 salespeople, most of them young and inexperienced. Brian owns up to "letting many of them down," but says he was just trying things. "The thing is—we just didn't know. Everybody expects the boss to know. But we were trying a lot of things, and some of them didn't work. One of the things that definitely did not work is hiring a lot of salespeople. And, therefore, we had high turnover."

Despite the high turnover and tough lessons, Sageworks more than doubled its revenue every year and created a successful company, "now that I look back on it with some perspective," Brian concludes. "The good news is that we were able to get revenue. But the bad news is that it was hard-fought-for revenue. Hard-won. Maybe with more strategic thinking, we could have ramped up our sales more quickly."

Where is Sageworks Now?

By 2017 Sageworks had expanded its customer base to thousands of CPA firms and financial institutions. According to Brian, "We're not two guys in a garage anymore, and we're now learning to grow as a larger company."

Despite Sageworks' high growth rate, it has actually reduced the size of its salesforce. Sageworks has matured and embraces stability and consistency instead of letting chaotic growth wash over it. In 2012, "Sageworks is a kinder, gentler nation," Brian says, "It's not just blindly bringing on people and firing them when they can't do the job."

In order to continue its growth, Sageworks is building "need-to-have" products that solve real problems versus offering "nice-to-have" solutions. It has added problem-solving software tools for banks including auditing, financial benchmarking, business projections, and credit processing. And Sageworks' products have come a long way since its failed partnership with the big bank, as much of its recent growth has come from banks.

Sageworks has also expanded its sales and marketing strategy beyond telemarketing and direct sales. "There are a lot of limits to the direct salesforce methodology," Brian explains. "And we became aware of them, eventually." For example, the company is building greater brand awareness and forging partnerships to find customers faster. And with greater brand awareness, it's deployed Web-based marketing techniques that have reduced the cost per sale.

Despite Sageworks' enormous success, Brian is operating on work-life balance instead of a growth-at-all-cost mentality, and it's working well.

Conclusion
In which grit is more than determination

Sunday Grit is a newspaper that for more than 120 years has catered to small-town, rural America. At its peak in 1969, it had more than 1.5 million subscribers and was the largest weekly family publication in the world.[22]

Its founder was 25-year-old German immigrant, Dietrick Lamade. In 1882 he was a foreman for a news publication, *Daily*

Sun and Banner, and its weekly publication, *Grit*, in Williamsport, Pennsylvania. But the publisher ran into financial troubles and needed to sell *Grit*.

Lamade and two financial partners gambled $1,100 to buy *Grit*. His plan for turning *Grit* around was to attract a wider audience by writing unique, "small town" features with good humor, patriotism, and religion.

In the beginning *Grit* couldn't pay its bills. Its circulation was only 4,000, and seven financial partners came and went.[23] But Lamade refused to give up and kept trying creative ideas to increase readership. For example, he devised a Thanksgiving Day raffle— offering to give away a rifle, a piano, and a bedroom suite to attract readership by including a raffle coupon with the paper. He travelled by train throughout northeastern Pennsylvania to persuade store owners and newsagents to carry his publication and promote his raffle. The raffle idea worked. Many people who purchased the paper for the free coupon also liked its stories.

Finally, after more than two years of tireless effort, Lamade increased circulation to 14,000, paid off his debts, and lived like an Horatio Alger hero. According to its website, the name *Grit* was fitting: "No one seems to know how the name *Grit* came to be. However, it not only was the paper's name, but sheer grit was how the newspaper survived those early years."[24]

Entrepreneurial grit is still one of the most important traits required to start and build an innovative business. The Panel Study of Entrepreneurial Development II database included 1,214 entrepreneurs, including follow-up interviews during a five-year period, to gain insight into how companies are created. The study revealed that after four years, two-thirds of the start-ups were still actively engaged in the start-up process, gaining traction by ample application of grit! Only 12-23% reported that they had an operating new firm after four years.[25]

Case in point is the creation of Xerox Corporation, a $21.6 billion company with 136,000 employees in 2010. Without gritty determination, the company probably wouldn't be the juggernaut it is today. Chester Carlson, who invented Xerox's flagship product, the modern-day copy machine, spent a great deal of his life turning his idea into a reality.

In 1934 Carlson worked in a patent department and became frustrated by reproducing his drawings several times over. In response, he set out to invent a device that could copy images.[26] It took him four years to make the first xerographic copy. By 1938 his prototype was a working machine and should have been ready to market and sell. But that didn't happen because Carlson didn't have the capital or experience to produce and distribute it.

Carlson spent four additional years asking twenty firms to help him develop and market his invention. They all turned him down. Finally, a nonprofit company agreed to help him. Three years later, Haloid Company obtained the commercial rights to his xerographic invention. Eleven years after that, Haloid-now calling itself Xerox—finally introduced the office copy machine, making Carlson a multi-millionaire.[27] However, from the time that Carlson imagined his invention until it became a viable product, twenty-four years had elapsed.

Chester Carlson, Dietrick Lamande, and Brian Hamilton's start-up stories show that building a viable business is messy, difficult work – in many ways more akin to blue-collar work than white-collar, "ivory-tower" work. Brian believes that most people have a difficult time relating to the degree of grit it takes to build a business.

Sageworks spent eighteen months building a product plus another two and a half years finding a market—CPA firms. That's four years grinding through grit for survival—and arrival. After that, he pushed an additional two years, from 2002 until 2004 trying to figure how best to sell to CPA firms.

What did Brian do during those six years? He mostly strategized to overcome discouraging events, losses, and bad decisions. That's determination. Brian kept fighting despite his long list of start-up challenges. And that's grit, the instinctual—then practical—bearing-down in the face of disappointments:

He invested $200,000 and spent 18 months creating financial formulas without a plan for who would buy them.

He experienced two false-positives, one from a big bank and one from a software firm, wherein partnerships he figured would be his big break fizzled into nothing.

He nearly ran out of money more than once. But instead of quitting or continuing to go through the motions, he drove across the country himself, looking for customers in order to "get some points on the board." That strategy worked for him when he discovered that CPAs were his best market.

His declared war on a multi-billion-dollar competitor. In doing so, he had to keep reacting to situations and challenges before him. Later, the bad results he got from overreacting taught him to modulate that impulsiveness into responding in the appropriate degree to challenges.

Grit: Perseverance and Passion for Long-Term Goals, by Angela Duckworth, et al., notes that many of the greatest professional accomplishments come from grit, not talent:

"In a qualitative study of the development of world-class pianists, neurologists, swimmers, chess players, mathematicians, and sculptors, Bloom (1985) noted that 'only a few of [the 120 talented individuals in the sample] were regarded as prodigies by teachers, parents, or experts.' (p. 533). Rather, accomplished individuals worked day after day, for at least 10 or 15 years, to reach the top of their fields."[28]

Sageworks' story teaches that entrepreneurial grit is often a greater competitive advantage than talent, planning, or education. Brian Hamilton has built a very successful company that not only employs hundreds but also has enabled hundreds of thousands of small businesses to be better interpreters of their own financial statements. And that's a measurable contribution, bringing more stability to the business climate.

So grit is more than just determination—it also derives power from its alternative meaning: hard, coarse-grained sandstone. Grit is messy. It takes on tough meetings, failed experiments, grinding slowly through ups and downs, getting there finally while others are left spinning their wheels, wasting their time and resources negotiating icy roads.

Chapter 4
iContact's Ryan Allis:
Using Kinetic Energy to Create Growth

One of the earliest known pictures of a hockey stick, shown below, was drawn by Englishman Francis Willughby (1635-1672).[29] To enjoy fully the competitive nature of the sport, he designed his stick with a blade at a sharp angle upward, topped by a shaft. Unlike Willughby's human-engineered version, a start-up's hockey stick-shaped growth curve is the result of many converging forces. Start-ups need a strong founder's force and energy during the Blade Years to be applied before sales growth becomes easier and easier to replicate in time. Then the game is on!

Francis Willughby's drawing of 1665 hockey stick

Introduction

iContact is a fast-growth company, today owned by PR Software firm Cision, whose product enables customers to create and send email newsletters, announcements, and promotions. The software is easy to use, so that small and medium-sized businesses with little technical ability can install and use it. iContact's software allows businesses to remain in touch with customers and prospective customers at the intervals they desire to be emailed, instead of being spammed daily. In 2012, iContact was sold to publicly-traded firm Cision for $169 million.

In 2003, when iContact started, email marketing software was in its infancy—only a few companies provided the service and hardly any businesses purchased it. But today email marketing software has become a big industry. An April 2012 report by Global Industry Analysts identifies 167 companies in the email marketing software industry.[30] Since that time, the industry has consolidated some, but there are still dozens of big players. iContact is often mentioned in media as a top provider along with publicly-traded rivals Constant Contact, as well as Mailchimp, ExactTarget and Vertical Response.

Co-founder and CEO Ryan Allis was an 18-year-old UNC-Chapel Hill freshman when he started iContact in 2003 with senior Aaron Houghton. Ryan's boyish face, brown hair, and medium build attest to his youth, but he carries himself with the dignity of a seasoned CEO. Ryan, after all, has been in business for sixteen years.

Aaron identified a need, came up with the idea, and created the software that became iContact when his fledgling Web design firm programmed an easy way for a mountain cottage owner to email her list of weekly renters about availability during the off-season.

A few months later, Aaron showed his email marketing program to Ryan at a University Entrepreneurship Club meeting. Ryan was amazed by the idea, and the two teamed to start iContact.

They started out with almost no capital and Ryan often worked from his dormitory room.

In this chapter two college students create a $50 million business in eight years. How they did that may surprise you, yet their process is eminently adoptable, in part or in whole, by other start-up founders.

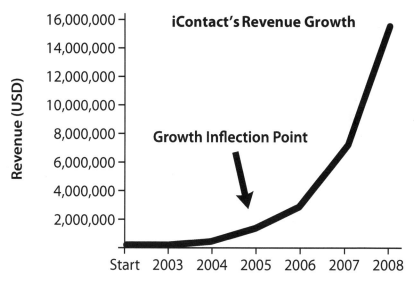

Kinetic Energy

While snow skiing at Park City, Utah, an 11-year-old boy practicing with his ski team flew by me travelling twice my speed.

"How do you get going so fast?" I asked while we rode the ski lift together.

"I get kinetic energy from pushing my outside ski one direction, and my body the other," the boy explained.

Kinetic energy is a form of energy that an object has by reason of its motion.

A giant meteor zooming through space, a locomotive headed down the tracks, or a marble rolling along the floor are all examples. Objects in motion possess their own energy.

The boy's skiing lesson also reveals that kinetic energy isn't magically produced. Applying force propels an object into movement. The boy's pushing his ski in the opposite direction of his body creates force. The directed propulsion creates motion and therefore kinetic energy. And the laws of physics tell us that the boy's body remains in motion, then, until something stops it—such as gravity, friction from the snow, or a tree.

The space shuttle blasting into orbit is another example of force moving an object, leading to the production of kinetic energy. When the shuttle is ready to launch, two rockets and an external fuel tank larger than the shuttle are attached to propel it for eight and half minutes after takeoff. The two rockets, filled with 500,000 kg of fuel, advance the shuttle twenty-eight miles above the earth. Then its external tank filled with 720,000 kg of liquid fuel propels the shuttle the next forty miles. The rockets and the external tanks, having done their jobs, are jettisoned from the shuttle into the ocean below.

Approximately seventy miles above earth, the shuttle reaches the required speed to orbit earth—approximately 17,500 miles per hour.[31] By that time it possesses kinetic energy equivalent to 900,000,000 watt-hours of energy—the electrical energy used by about 300,000 homes in one day! The space shuttle now has adequate energy to spend several days orbiting the earth while using little fuel in comparison with its speed and length of time in space.[32]

The principles of kinetic energy apply to entrepreneurship as well. The founder applies great force to launch a start-up, but once the company is launched, the company's own repeated, self-generated motion in the marketplace supplies energy that helps the business grow.

Skipping Class ... To Do Marketing

While living in Bradenton, Florida, in 1995 at age eleven, Ryan received his first computer from his uncle. He took to it immediately, soon starting his own business repairing computers during the summer. He promoted the fledging business by stuffing flyers into mailboxes, but his first call came from the postmaster, telling him to stop putting them in mailboxes without stamps. The boy earned $463 that summer – good money for a twelve-year-old.

In middle school Ryan learned HTML, software code used to create websites. One of his first clients imported jewelry from China, and he helped her use the Internet to find customers. She had a good idea but couldn't manage her business operations – like inventory, orders, customer service, and supply chain. That experience of watching her good business fail had a profound impact on Ryan—he realized that having a good product wasn't enough to make a good company viable.

While in high school, Ryan launched Viranté - a Web design and development company. It set up websites and e-commerce integrations for a medical care company, a dating service, a travel agency, and others. He learned about invoicing, strategic partnerships, public relations, and running a small business. But Ryan's real interest was online marketing, and he spent a great deal of time reading about and learning it.

When Ryan was a high school senior, a client who had developed a treatment for arthritis recognized Ryan's internet skills and hired him as VP of Marketing. Ryan convinced his high school to let him get class credit for an internship he did during the last two periods each day. He worked at the company's office each day from noon until 7 p.m. marketing the treatment via the web.

Though Ryan helped it grow from a tiny operation to over $1 million in sales in just over a year, he recalls, "I didn't yet realize

I was an entrepreneur—I viewed myself as a marketer, but what I was learning about financing, payroll, bank relations, product positioning, and human resources would help me tremendously when I did set out to be an entrepreneur myself."

Ryan not only learned about running a business, he also learned how internet marketing worked when it was still in its infancy. He was only 17 years old, yet he had control over a $50,000-per-month marketing budget. Through trial and error he learned a great deal about marketing and using the internet to find customers.

When Ryan graduated from high school in 2002, he faced a dilemma—should he go to college or not? "I thought I had the skills and resources to succeed without college. And I feared that college would prepare me to work for someone else, even though I knew that I didn't want to work for anyone but myself."

But Ryan also wanted a social life and the college experience, so he decided to move away from home and attend the University of North Carolina at Chapel Hill. "I was not sure that I could survive the psychological stress of being 18 and not having a single friend younger than 27," Ryan said.

So Ryan packed his bags and headed to North Carolina, but he kept his web consulting business, Viranté, going at the same time.

An Idea Is Conceived

On October 2, 2002, as a college freshman, Ryan joined UNC's Entrepreneurship Club. At one of their meetings he met Aaron Houghton, a senior computer science major. Aaron, like Ryan, had an established web design company, Preation, Inc. The two had a lot in common, so they met a few days later to exchange ideas.

Aaron was a talented programmer. He had developed several web-related products – an online calendar, an affiliate marketing tool, and an email tool. But the tool that caught Ryan's eye was an

Email Newsletter Sender. Aaron's customer Michelle McMahan, of Mountain Brook Cottages, wanted an easy way to email her customers during the off-season. To the best of Aaron's knowledge, an efficient system that sends bulk emails didn't exist at the time—so he built one for Michelle.

Ryan had experienced trouble in sending bulk email newsletters to customers when marketing the arthritis treatment in high school, so both he and Aaron wanted to solve the problem.

"The company I had worked with in my senior year in high school used a desktop-based program called Mailloop to send out their email newsletter," Ryan explained. "It would often take 24 hours or more for a newsletter to be sent, completely tying up all the resources of a company computer during this time.

"The software Aaron had developed, however, was web-based, meaning that it could be accessed from any computer with an internet connection anywhere in the world; once you composed your message and hit *send,* you would be done right away. You could close your browser and go to other work while the server sent out the emails within a matter of minutes.

"Aaron's software had some other features that made it unique, such as automatically tracking opens and clicks. At the entry level, Aaron's product idea cost only $10 per month rather than the $400 up-front cost of Mailloop. It was simply a better solution, and, since my entrepreneurial mind is always running, I saw possibilities immediately."

Organizing iContact

In February 2003, Ryan and Aaron decided to work together to market Aaron's email sender to other small businesses. If Mountain Brook Cottages needed the tool and would pay good money for it, then why wouldn't others? The potential seemed unlimited because millions of small businesses like Mountain Brook Cottages need a professional way to contact their customers and prospects via email.

Ryan and Aaron called their product IntelliContact, later changing it to iContact. Ryan said they started out a bit naïve but that their ignorance may have helped them.

"When we first started, I'm really glad I didn't know what I know now. Otherwise, I might not have done it, you know? Sometimes a little bit of naïveté or even ignorance helps because when you don't know how hard it's going to be, you're definitely going to do it."

For example, Ryan said if he had started now, he would have more thoroughly investigated the competition, which might have persuaded him not to start iContact because, as it turned out, several other entrepreneurs had had the same idea – even before Ryan and Aaron did.

"I wasn't aware of some of the competitors. If I had been, we might have come to the conclusion 'This solution already exists in the market so what's the purpose of creating something new?' Being a little ignorant as far as competitors [went] was very helpful," Ryan recalls.

In the beginning IntelliContact operated as a joint venture between their firms—Viranté for marketing and Preation for product development. Three months later, Ryan's professor recommended that they create one company so there would be greater organization, less time expended in admin, and financial clarity.

While most 18 and 21-year-olds were caught up in fraternity and sorority rush, intramural sports, classes, and drinking games – Ryan and Aaron negotiated corporate legal agreements to start iContact.

Ryan would be CEO and Aaron Chairman of the Board and CTO. They decided that Aaron should own more of the new company's stock since he had written the product. They offered shares to employees working on the project as well, since iContact was paying them less than market-rate salaries. Today Ryan wishes he had placed more value on his own equity when organizing iContact.

"I wish I had known how valuable equity is and not given it away so easily. We gave our first employee seven percent of the company. Fortunately, we vested him over four years, so when he left eight months later he only got 1½ percent. Theoretically, it was worth little then, but it ended up being worth a lot. Our second employee got 15 percent and he vested the whole thing.

"I wish I'd had a better ability to translate equity into what the potential value might be down the road so we hadn't unnecessarily diluted ourselves as much early on. I should have explained, 'What do you think the proper compensation would be for four or five years of work? Maybe a million bucks a year, risk adjusted?'

"But not three million bucks a year! That [generous degree of] equity was critical in our ability to attract people and keep people on staff because we were paying under-market salaries. Even so, our first two to four employees got a lot."

By August 2003 they had agreed upon and signed thirty-three legal documents. Clearly, Ryan and Aaron weren't treating iContact as a pet project, but rather as a real business.

Ryan also wrote a business plan for their new company, but today he says that most start-ups don't need full-fledged, detailed business plans.

"Don't worry about the business plan," Ryan says. "Just create an execution plan; create a marketing plan; create a go-to market plan; create an operations plan. But don't worry about a business plan; it's all made up, anyway. It's good to do the research and understand your market, but I see a lot of entrepreneurs create a 45-page plan and I'm just sort of like, why? Create a 20-page

PowerPoint doc; that's all you need. And just go at it. Give your product away for free to get feedback from users; [then] make your product better, incorporating the feedback when it's useful."

Disillusioned by College

As a college freshman, Ryan wasn't settling for taking typical prerequisite classes. He wanted an applicable, strategic business education instead. With help from UNC's Center for Entrepreneurship, based upon his unusual background, he was permitted to pursue an independent study in entrepreneurship.

The independent study enabled him to attend the M.B.A. classes "Venture Capital Deal Structure" and "Legal Issues for High Technology Start-ups," among others. He interviewed six experienced entrepreneurs and completed other related projects. All of this was valuable, but Ryan found it tough to balance so many activities.

"The hard part was I was still going to school. I had to balance taking a full college workload with running a start-up business. iContact wasn't generating revenue yet. But it was generating expenses, for sure, in terms of servers and hosting. And I was doing some consulting, web-marketing consulting work, search-engine optimization through my company, Viranté. I was able to make three or four thousand dollars a month that I could live off of and invest in the new venture."

Let's recap. At eighteen, during his second semester of freshman year, Ryan was a full-time student taking M.B.A. classes, launching iContact with Aaron, and in his "spare time" doing web consulting and bringing in $3,000 - $4,000 a month.

"I didn't know a lot of people, and certainly there are not a lot of people who were like me, entrepreneurial. I was pretty different from the average eighteen-year-old."

Ryan had a strong pull towards action and making things work. He hated illogical, cover-all-eventualities rules. For example, college administrators' response to his running a business from his dorm room lit him up.

"I got a letter in my dorm saying I was using the dorm for commercial purposes and that if I continued to do so, they [would] kick me out of school. That's the silliest thing I've ever heard! You'd think a school would want to encourage their students to be entrepreneurs. But there was still that old mentality that academics and business are opposite things—that business was about profiting, instead of making a difference in people's lives and creating value for others. I wanted to take action; I didn't want to talk about stuff all day. I wanted to do something."

In May 2003, Ryan dropped out of college to pursue iContact. He wanted to do business, not talk about it: "I wanted to go build a business; that's what I had learned how to do and what I was really passionate about."

Other successful entrepreneurs have dropped out of college as well. Bill Gates left Harvard after his sophomore year and, according to Malcolm Gladwell's book, *Outliers*, dropping out provided Gates with the extra time needed to practice software programming and launch Microsoft at the perfect time.[33] Larry Elison, CEO and founder of $35-billion revenue Oracle Software, attended the Universities of Illinois and Chicago, but got degrees from neither.

Sir Richard Branson, who started and owns Virgin and who is one of the world's most famous entrepreneurs, ended his formal education in public school at sixteen. His headmaster's parting words were, "Congratulations, Branson. I predict that you will either go to prison or become a millionaire."[34] Branson did neither—he became a billionaire and today owns his own island.

Getting iContact off the Ground

Force is needed to produce kinetic energy. Likewise, a startup company requires force to produce the energy to become viable. But most start-ups have few resources so founders must provide that force. Like launching the space shuttle, the most force is required *up front*—unfortunate, because the beginning is typically when the smallest amount of resources is available. Start-ups have few employees, little capital, no customers referring other customers, no systems or processes, and no success creating more success. They just have an idea. This is what makes starting a new business difficult; thus without a good idea, start-ups have close to nothing.

In 2003, iContact's first year in business, it sold $11,964 worth of product and had $17,000 in expenses. Ryan was discouraged. "We had worked a year of our lives to lose $5,000."

iContact was like millions of other start-ups with a shoestring budget, watching every nickel to make ends meet. The company had little money for food—much less for product development and marketing.

"I remember going down to UNC Surplus for a $20 desk and a $40 computer," Ryan recalls. "I remember eating at the same sushi restaurant day after day where you can get six pieces of sushi for a dollar. I remember sitting in the hallway working because we ran out of space. I remember jumping in dumpsters to get proof-of-purchase tags off our chair boxes to get the $50 rebates at Staples."

Ryan and Aaron invested as much as they could into iContact, but still they couldn't afford what iContact needed. For example, late in 2003 it lost customers because its server broke and it couldn't afford a backup server. "We were offline for a week and a half and lost 35 percent of our customers because of that," Ryan says.

The first year was a brutal surprise for Ryan. Remember, in high school as a VP of Marketing, he had helped build a $1 million business in less than a year.

"The business from high school went from two thousand during month one, to two hundred thousand during month twelve. But the difference was the founder had spent three years getting the product ready, so that in month one, our product was solid. Whereas, in month one for us, the product was definitely not solid—we had to spend a year getting the product to a place where it was suitable for mass consumption."

For example, in February 2003 when iContact launched, it didn't have bounce–back handling, so if an email was invalid, the sender wouldn't know it. That was one of the first features iContact added, in July 2003.

iContact also needed to find out what unique features the market wanted. But it, like many new innovative products, fell into a catch-22. iContact couldn't get feedback because it couldn't sell the product. It couldn't sell the product because it couldn't get feedback. So Ryan used his common sense to dig out— he gave iContact's product away for free and begged users for feedback in return.

"We gave the product away for free to local restaurants to get some usage, awareness, and feedback. A lot of entrepreneurs skip answering: 'How do you get some sales going initially?' It took a lot of hard work and a lot of guerilla marketing tactics to get people to use the product."

iContact could afford to give away its product for free because it had no variable costs. Most of its costs were up front in building the system. Adding users was cheap so giveaways didn't cost much, and the feedback was invaluable.

"Gradually, over time we were able to invest more in research and development. We added additional features, like a surveying tool, an auto-responder tool. We added a lot more templates, so that people could get professionally designed templates for their messages."

Internet marketing had been Ryan's unique skill. During the first year he invested thousands of hours of sweat equity leveraging the internet to find customers. One of Ryan's strategies was getting affiliates, who'd promote iContact to find their own paying customers. His affiliate program enabled other website owners to refer business to iContact for a commission. iContact used technology to track the referrals.

"We couldn't afford salespeople so we did web marketing. I tried to get as many customers as possible without spending a lot of money. The great thing about the reseller and affiliate programs is that you pay out only after a sale is made. You already have the money in your bank account before you write the check for the commissions, completely eliminating risk for [yourself]."

iContact made the affiliate program easy and attractive in order to help convince websites that it was good for them. Another way Ryan created marketing awareness was by convincing other websites to link to iContact – improving its presence on Google.

"The entire summer of 2003 was all about getting links from other websites to link to us, so we could get #1 in Google for email marketing software. Because once you have that, it's free traffic. We set up five or six hundred links that summer. Maybe more."

Ryan's sales and marketing programs worked to increase iContact's revenue. From the month Ryan had dropped out of college, May 2003, forward, his marketing online programs helped sales improve from $500 a month to $20,000 a month by August of 2004. Revenue in 2004, the second year, was $296,000.[35] Despite the increase, Ryan remained disappointed because iContact didn't take off as he had hoped.

"We hadn't made quite as much progress as I thought we

would. I just thought it would go faster. We only had six or eight employees when I went back to school. I felt I could manage both. I wasn't sure iContact was going to make it, so I hedged my bets and made sure I could get a college degree as well as build a company."

Common sense told Ryan that if a product was really good, its sales would take off and grow fast. His biggest surprise came in seeing how long it took to get customers and thus to ramp up revenue.

"It took twice as long, or three times as long, to get to a million dollars in revenue. It took three years, and I thought it'd take a year and a half."

Ryan, glancing off into space, softly laughs at himself – most likely reliving the insanity—the delusion—of it all.

"I think it almost always takes longer than you think to build a business. That's why most entrepreneurs don't make it, initially. They think it's going to take a year, and really it takes three years. And if you're not willing to put in three years, it's questionable whether you should start."

iContact Builds Energy

Why does it take such a long time to develop a market? Ryan explains that momentum, which takes a long time to build up, is a key element in starting an innovative company.

"You need all the same processes to get to fifty thousand in monthly revenue that you needed to get to ten thousand. But, when you're at zero, you have nothing; when you're at ten thousand, you got a heck of a lot that you can take advantage of to get to fifty thousand."

"You have to figure out how to generate revenue without generating expenses. You have to find creative, inexpensive ways to market so that people can sign up and pay you money without [your] spending a lot in advertising."

To build momentum, Ryan and Aaron made sacrifices like not taking salaries in 2004 despite having adequate revenue, $296,000, to do so. Instead of taking salaries, they plowed revenue back into the company by investing first in customer service and marketing.

"Those first dollars of revenue went into hiring a customer-service person to handle the phones. After covering that expense each month, every dollar went into Google AdWords, the foundation of iContact's early marketing strategy," said Aaron in a July 10, 2010, *Inc. Magazine* article, "30 under 30: America's Coolest Young Entrepreneurs," by Matt Quinn.[36]

Paid advertising on Google gave iContact a new, revenue-generating marketing vehicle for finding customers. Then, iContact's marketing strategy of paying Google and other advertisers a per-click fee helped it grow its customer base efficiently. Ryan began to feel kinetic energy pulling iContact foward—he was making iContact work "on its own" and privately starting to believe in it.

iContact's next investment was a key hire to improve its product. "In February 2004 we had a really critical hire, David Rasch, who is still with us today as chief architect and CTO. He enabled us to improve the product in a way that made a big impact on the company."

Ryan and Aaron's wise investments and the sacrifices they made by investing in iContact instead of paying themselves made an impact. With sales ramping up in 2005, Ryan decided to quit college again and run iContact full-time.

"By the end of that second year in college in May of 2005, we were at $60,000 - $70,000 a month in sales with about twelve employees. I needed to be there full time."

Ryan's job during the first two and half years had been to get customers to sign up without his spending a lot of money, to learn what features the product needed, and to manage a small staff. He had worked very hard to make iContact viable. And now that iContact was becoming larger, Ryan's job was about to become more complex. He needed to learn something new – how to raise funds to grow.

iContact had bootstrapped to startup, using inexpensive, creative tactics to build sales without outside money. Its revenue was $11,964 in 2003; $296,000 in 2004; $1.3 million in 2005; $2.9 million in 2006.[37]

By 2005, it had mastered proven techniques that could be repeated for greater success. iContact was hitting its growth inflection point. At this point the "art" of creating a business becomes more a science. For example, iContact mastered cost-per-click marketing techniques to the point that whenever they invested a dollar into the program, they knew how much money they'd get in return from landing new customers.

By 2005 they could likely have sold iContact for at least $3-5 million if not more—making Ryan and Aaron millionaires before twenty-five. And Ryan had already met his initial goal of running a $1 million company.

"My goal since age eighteen had been to build a company to $1 million in sales before my 21st birthday. ...We hit the milestone on September 1, 2005. I missed my deadline by eighteen days, but I was still elated. ... We had to make the choice whether to sell the company or raise outside capital to grow further. We chose to begin the process of raising funding."[38]

Keeping the dream alive, Ryan and Aaron had researched the email-marketing market and figured it had enormous potential. Roughly 30 million small businesses operate in the U.S., but only a few hundred thousand had adopted email marketing tools. Ryan and Aaron wanted to capture more of that open market. Loving the challenge, they decided to pursue acquiring capital to grow iContact themselves.

iContact Learns to How Acquire Capital

In October 2005, two and a half years after its inception, iContact began raising capital to grow. Ryan had no experience doing so, but he knew the first offer wasn't a good one. A well-known venture fund valued iContact at $6 million – well below what he and Aaron believed it was worth. "We tried to raise capital the first time and it didn't work," Ryan said. "We weren't happy with the terms that we got, so we turned them down."

Ryan looked for someone who could help them negotiate the complex world of venture capital (VC).

"We had never raised capital before, so we didn't know what things like 'participating preferred' and 'liquidation preferences' were. And we just thought 'valuation' was valuation—didn't really understand the difference between a structured term sheet and a straight term sheet."

iContact hired an experienced CFO, Tim Oakley, to represent them in finding the best possible deal. Oakley had been through the fundraising process several times and he had helped oversee the sale of businesses worth more than $500 million.

"We hired Tim Oakley, a great negotiator, so having him on the team added that stamp of credibility we needed to get the round done. He helped us negotiate the best possible deal and got us a deal done for $500,000 of convertible debt that ended up converting a year later into equity, into a $16 million valuation."

iContact raised $500,000 in seed-round financing from N.C. Idea, a deal that converted debt to equity according to an agreed upon formula. But it took them longer than they had anticipated to close the deal.

"It was pretty contentious. We started in October of 2005, thinking it might take us five or six months, but it took nine months. It certainly took us longer than expected to raise capital."

The new money meant iContact was no longer dependent upon itself for growth – it was now in a position to use outside capital and grow much faster. Ryan was evolving from being a scrappy entrepreneur who did things himself into being the leader of a complex, growing organization. He was proving his evolution through actions like having the insight to admit he needed help raising money and then convincing an experienced CFO like Tim Oakley to join iContact. Smart actions like those attract venture capitalists.

Acquiring venture capital is very competitive, but VCs like to invest in companies like iContact where a thriving product exists in a large, mainly untapped market. VC general partners look at management talent as much as or more than they do products. In a speech at a recent venture capital conference, one partner said, "We look for talent, talent, talent, repeat five times," "We look for experienced management at the corporate level," and "We look for great CEOs and inventory them." Another said, "We look for CEOs obsessed with how their product fits in with strategic buyers." In other words, they look for CEOs who think about who is going to buy the company down the road—and why, then work to bring their fledgling company up to specifications.

Ed McCarthy, a venture capitalist with River Cities Capital, explains what a typical VC might look for when making an investment.

"Our investment profile is generally entrepreneurs who have already gotten through a couple of gates. So they're not the ones that are three guys, a dog, and an idea in a garage. They've already gotten up to a million, two million, three million, five million in revenue—but every investment is different."

In 2011 of the 3,673 U.S. venture capital deals, only 396 of those were "seed" or "first-round" investments. The rest were "early-stage," "expansion," or "later-stage" investments.[39]

Ed said that the typical leader of a VC-backed company is a team player, not defensive or controlling, and that he or she drives value for shareholders:

"He is driven; he can articulate the vision and what he wants to accomplish. He must be willing to, and want to, work with investors. He wants to get some outside viewpoints and assistance in terms of advice, governance, introductions, and different ways to approach things. And he's willing to give up some of the control.

"His motivation is to drive great value and take advantage of an opportunity in a timely way because time is of the essence. For the entrepreneur who chooses the path of organic growth, of bootstrapping, it is great, and he's retained his control that he found so precious, but [by taking so much time] he may allow [new competitors] to say, 'I'm going to do that [idea], too.'"

Ryan is the type of driven team leader Ed looks for. Ryan focuses on leading, not on having to run areas of the business himself.

Ryan advises growth and value-oriented entrepreneurs to "hire people with more experience than you, [people] who are smarter than you in their particular area, [people] who can do their jobs much, much better than you. Train them; trust but verify; and then trust and let them go [to work].

"I try to let myself scale. So, if we hire people who can run their areas, who can manage their operations, I can focus on culture, on investment, on strategy, and on people," Ryan said. "My ideas don't matter anymore. For the most part I'm selling the company; I'm selling the future profitability and annuity-revenue stream that the company will generate if we execute on our strategy.

"Some people may want to build a lifestyle business where they're in control of operations, and they get to make every decision down to the minutest detail. But as long as there's conscious understanding, the downside of that is that your business will not

scale, and it will not grow beyond your own ability to produce."
Today Ryan works long hours but loves his job. He recently
tweeted at 3:00 a.m.: "Somebody planned a bfast panel, 2 board
mtgs, and a Q3 kickoff mtg in 36 hours :). I think I just worked
from 8am to 230am, loving it though."

Ryan's hard work and leadership skills have helped iContact continue to raise capital to grow. From 2006 to 2009, it raised
nearly $18 million, approximately five million each year. The
company invested the dollars into repeatable, profitable processes.

"The whole business is based upon a mathematical model
where we invest $500 to acquire a customer, and can get $2,500
to $2,600 in lifetime revenue," Ryan explains. "So it takes about
eleven, twelve months to pay back that up-front investment. And
then that turns into three years of gross profit after that.

"It's online advertising, basically. We spend about $1.5 million
a month to acquire about 3,000 customers a month. And we just
keep doing that over and over and over, and it's a very profitable
model. So we have a choice now to start making the company
churn out cash and become very profitable, or raise more money
to get even more aggressive."

By 2010 iContact was confident it could continue growing because the market is so large. It hired Allen & Company, a New
York City-based investment bank with a rich history of helping
successful online businesses like Google raise capital. In August
2010, JMI Equity, a Baltimore-based growth equity firm, invested
$40 million in iContact. JMI Equity has invested more than $2.1
billion into 100 previous investments, including Double Click, acquired by Google, and publicly traded software firm Blackbaud.

After iContact closed on the investment, *The News & Observer* quoted venture capitalist Merrette Moore complimenting Ryan's management ability: "Ryan has what it takes to get to whatever level they want to get to. His vision and cult of personality

are a big part of that."[40]

Ryan was now benefitting from the kinetic energy created in the beginning by his and Aaron's diligent, consistent pushing for product superiority and marketing appeal.

iContact Today

In February 2012 iContact was acquired for $169 million by Cision, a company that provides a wide range of marketing solutions for small and medium-sized businesses. In a blog post to customers after the merger, Ryan said:

iContact has come a long way from our early days in Chapel Hill and Durham. Aaron and I as co-founders have learned a key lesson along the way—if you surround yourself with smart, caring, and passionate people and focus on creating value for customers, employees, and the community, amazing things can happen.[41]

On March 20, 2012, Ryan resigned from iContact, and in August 2012 began graduate work at Harvard Business School. He has also started another company, Connect, software that will connect people globally. Ryan started Hive, an energetic community of 1,100 CEOs dedicated to helping create a better world.

Ryan also wants to help end poverty through business investment. "My *only* goal in life is to help end extreme poverty in our lifetime," Ryan says. "I've been to Uganda twice, to Kenya, and to Ethiopia. Going to East Africa opened my eyes to the need and the great opportunity."

Rather than long-term government aid and subsidies, Ryan's solution for helping to end extreme poverty is based upon investing in African for-profit companies.

"In ten years I want to be running the largest socially responsible hedge fund in Africa. I don't think the solution is government-to-government aid. A big part of the solution is investing in local entrepreneurs who create jobs, who pay tax revenue, who hold their government accountable for education, healthcare, roads, and infrastructure. Not a lot of people invest between $5,000 and $100,000 in equity in African entrepreneurs. We need to take it from the $50 - $100 loan up to the $5,000 investment, a $20,000 investment, a $100,000 investment.

"There's a tremendous, very profitable business opportunity investing in small and medium-sized African businesses. The average per capita income in Africa today is $800, which was where the United States was 200 years ago. Wouldn't you [want to] have invested in the United States in 1810?"

Conclusion
In which kinetic energy helps start-ups —
if the founder keeps pushing.

Amazon, in 2015 a $107 billion online retailer, was started in 1994 by entrepreneur Jeff Bezos. Growing up working on his grandfather's farm in South Texas taught Bezos independence and self-sufficiency.[42] He studied electrical engineering and computer science at Princeton, graduating with a 4.2 GPA in 1984. Bezos also had a knack for business and dreamed of starting his own.

In 1994 while working for financial data software firm D.E. Shaw, founder David Shaw asked Bezos to look into creating sales for the company by means of a new phenomenon—the internet. Bezos showed him an industry with huge potential: selling books online, but Shaw rejected Jeff's idea because it wasn't related to financial software. So Bezos struck out on his own.

According to Richard Brandt's *One Click: Jeff Bezos and the Rise of Amazon.com*, Amazon was a bare-bones start-up. Bezos hired two programmers and paid them with stock and salary. Bezos made the first investment: $10,000 to buy stock and $44,000 in loans. His wife, MacKenzie, handled phone calls, ordering, accounting, and administration. Amazon's first office in Seattle was the garage of an $890/month rental house, and its second office was a 1,100 sq/ft. space "shared with a needle exchange program and a shuttered pawn shop."[43]

Bezos had a lot to learn about books, so he attended a class on how to open a bookstore. One of the class's instructors, Richard Howorth, of Square Books, in Oxford, Mississippi, said Bezos was silent about his project but anxious to to learn. "I could tell he was doing some deep thinking about it, a lot of planning."[44]

Trial-and-error was Amazon's initial game plan. "We made some good guesses and a lot of poor ones," said Paul Davis, one of Amazon's first employees.[45]

For example, one of Amazon's biggest start-up challenges was figuring out how to show consumers millions of book titles for sale without having to maintain expensive inventory. They figured it out by creating technology that enabled Amazon to order from distributors as soon as the customer ordered a book.

Building an online platform and database took Bezos and his programmers about a year. In 1995 when it launched its online store, Amazon heavily discounted books, resulting in big financial losses, but Bezos figured the discounts would provide word-of-mouth marketing to make Amazon a household name.

In the beginning tasks had to be done manually that he knew should have been automated. For example, each week they manually copied and pasted millions of book titles from CDs into the database. Also, Amazon's first employees wore kneepads to pack books on a concrete floor. Employee Nicholas Lovejoy suggested to Bezos that he buy packing tables instead of kneepads. "I thought that was the most brilliant idea I had ever heard in my life,"[46] Bezos said. Seems they were moving faster to process orders than they could think.

Despite Amazon's having to work out some initial kinks, it learned to offer customers simple yet appealing features that made the site not only a popular website but also a necessary one. "If you want to be successful in the short-to-medium term, you can only do things that offer incredibly strong value propositions to customers relative to the value of doing things in more traditional ways," Jeff says about the early years.[47]

Amazon's strong value proposition included offering customers a wide range of titles, deep discounts, and easy-to-navigate technology to help customers find the books they wanted. Those foundations provided Amazon with early-adopter customers who spread the word for them. And soon media like the *Wall Street Journal* and Yahoo! noticed Amazon's convenient website and they also promoted it. Then, to take advantage of the momentum, Amazon started offering commissions to other websites that linked to books in Amazon's database.

Amazon's marketing and its strong value proposition helped its revenue growth form a game-winning hockey-stick trajectory: $0 in 1994, $511,000 in 1995, $15 million in 1996, $147 million in 1997, $610 million in 1998, and $1.6 billion in 1999. It expanded product offerings in 1998 by selling music and movies and in 1999 electronics.

Amazon's start-up story resembles a space shuttle launch—a tremendous amount of inefficient, founder-provided force upfront, then leveraging that force to create kinetic energy. Jeff Bezos's delayed efforts to switch from kneepads to packing tables in 1994 and 1995 may seem unsophisticated, but his enormous, dedicated sweat equity upfront created motion for Amazon and moved his good idea forward fast.

Bezos did the very best he could with the limited resources he had. He leveraged his strength, computer programming knowledge, as the initial force that enabled Amazon to move. Not until

1996 did kinetic energy take hold, but then revenues expanded exponentially and a snowball effect ensued.

Good ideas like Amazon become successful businesses partly because initial small success breeds bigger successes. Sales have an ability to produce their own sales. Product improvements follow from more and more user feedback. Success has a way of staying in motion—rather as kinetic energy keeps an object in motion.

An innovative company must create force to generate motion at the start. In the first year iContact had to exert tremendous effort just to move revenues from $0 to $11,964 because of common barriers like the product's inadequacies, the lack of capital, lack of customers, lack of marketing history, and management inexperience. Creativity, hard work, and willingness to adapt one's good idea with focus and determination helped Ryan overcome his early struggles to set iContact in motion.

Oftentimes, though, focused hard work doesn't pay off immediately, and that can be frustrating and difficult. For example, Ryan was so frustrated after the first 18 months that he thought his business was floundering, so he went back to college as his "plan B." But eventually creative forces like the ones below take hold, and the founders eventually do succeed:

Ryan offered free trials to potential users to obtain the critical feedback he needed to know what features to add, such as survey tools and email design templates.

Ryan dropped out of college in order to devote full-time efforts to iContact for little or no pay.

Ryan invested tremendous time in convincing websites to provide a link to iContact, helping improve its search-engine ranking.

In 2004 neither Ryan nor Aaron took salaries, instead plowing revenue into the business.

To find customers, Ryan established an affiliate marketing

program that paid commissions to any approved website referring paying customers to iContact.

In 2005 iContact hired David Rasch as a key technology partner to build sophisticated technology enabling it to become a product leader.

These creative forces provided by iContact's founders eventually did pay off. For iContact, as for Amazon, momentum is illustrated by a hockey-stick-shaped revenue growth curve. Its first year's revenue was $11,964, its second year's was $296,000, its third year's $1.3 million, and its fourth year's $2.9 million. iContact took three years to grow from $0 to $1 million, but it needed only five additional years to grow from $1 million to $50 million.

By 2006 iContact was benefitting from its own motion, like the space shuttle orbiting the earth on its kinetic energy. Ryan then focused on guiding his company, already in motion, to hire experienced managers to execute specific decisions and steer the ship.

iContact took advantage of its forward motion to raise $5 million three years in a row – 2007, 2008, and 2009. And in 2011, it raised $40 million. By then, iContact had mastered a repeatable model and Ryan had proved himself to be a VC-ready leader. Most important fact of all, however: Ryan and Aaron wanted to make the sacrifices necessary to grow into a larger company.

Just because a start-up gets to the point of benefitting from its own motion, that doesn't mean it doesn't face challenges. Kinetic energy is slowed by friction—like gravity slowing a runner trekking uphill, or wind blowing against a mosquito's wings, or a train's wheels abrading the tracks. In business, frictional forces like competition, difficult customers, product deficiencies, lawsuits, weak customer service, and poor management slow down growing companies. All growing companies must minimize friction to keep growing. Therefore, they need to apply continuous force to propel their companies—just as the space shuttle must still burn some fuel while orbiting earth above gravitational and atmospheric drag.

Once a company is viable, it doesn't need such tremendous manual force from its founder for its most basic functions. The differential effort it takes to obtain a prospective client lead is an example. Once a business is launched, instead of having only 30 prospective client leads, it may have 30,000 leads. Yet the founder's effort (or force) expended to obtain each lead is astronomically lower for obtaining the 30,000th lead than for obtaining the 30th lead. The business is now using forward motion for success, not the founder's energy to generate more success.

His deep knowledge of the long and constant fight against drag and friction causes Ryan to say that starting a business is challenging. "It's really, really hard to get [a new company] moving, but once you get it moving …that enables you to make it move faster. It gets easier and easier," Ryan says.

Ryan's comment also pertains to the launch of the space shuttle…except for one critical exception: the time it requires to get a company launched versus the time it takes to launch the shuttle. The shuttle requires only *eight and a half minutes* to launch and benefit from its intrinsic kinetic energy.[48] But a new company isn't so lucky in having the forces of nature always at the ready. It often takes years to turn a new idea into a thriving company. And human doubt and second-guessing can exert strong drag on a business—a factor the orbiting shuttle is not slowed by.

When I asked Ryan why so many entrepreneurs quit or fail after only a year, his advice pointed to patience and persistence. "Because humans, psychologically, have a tendency to overestimate what they can accomplish in one year, and underestimate what they can accomplish in ten years."

So iContact's trajectory illustrates a profound lesson for entrepreneurs: keep pushing the product and marketing forward.

Chapter 5
Graham Snyder's SEAL Innovation: Objectifying and Transforming Frustration into Creation

In physics, work is force applied to move or displace an object. For example, a hockey player creates work when striking a puck with a stick's blade. So in hockey, the blade is the *launching point* where work is created. For a start-up, the blade is the extended launching point at which a company begins to move.  During the Blade Years the founder conceptualizes, designs, and creates his or her innovative product. He also applies continuous force along the blade-as-time. What special skills do founders have to help them produce such work?

Introduction

Graham Snyder has created a patented invention that helps prevent children from drowning – a device called SwimSafe. The invention, ten years in the making, was first conceptualized in 2006, and now in 2016 is a reliable, working product.

The SwimSafe joins two devices: a transmitter and a receiver. The transmitter, a small box less than the size of a pack of gum, attaches to a necklace the child wears while swimming and determines whether he or she is at risk of drowning. The transmitter sends signals to the receiver, the second device. The receiver remains with lifeguards or guardians and monitors the child's safety. If the child is under water a few seconds longer than expected, the receiver buzzes and displays a yellow warning light. A few seconds later, the receiver sets off an all-around alarm—like a fire alarm.

Graham Snyder looks like an actor on the TV series ER. At five feet nine, he's slim and fit, with a shaved head, a goatee, and dark, rectangular glasses. Lively and animated, he's a 43-year-old emergency-room physician in Raleigh, N.C. Graham loves his work, but he dreads summertime.

Drownings: The Only Regularly Scheduled Deaths

"Summer's coming, and they'll be coming again," Graham says. Drownings are the only regularly scheduled deaths we have. The number one cause of death for children under five is drowning, yet children aren't supposed to die. "E.R. docs are sick of it, we want it to stop!" Graham exclaims.

"It doesn't have to happen, either. You know how small backyard pools are? They're ridiculously small, but a common place for a party – like a family picnic. You got the whole family in the pool. People are grilling, kids are doing cannonballs—it's great! And then one of the parents looks up and sees one of the kids on the bottom of the pool. They pull her up but she's dead. She just slipped under. And the thing was . . . the girl knew how to swim.

"But knowing how to swim is one thing when you're an ironman triathlete who swims in the ocean, but knowing how to swim when you're seven but you get water up your nose and then you cry and you can't see, and then you choke and then your legs are pinwheeling—that's something else. It seems like you're yelling for help really, really loud – but you're not. Your panic and death struggle is almost utterly silent when a lot of people are socializing around you. Her family couldn't hear her at all."

Graham also sees that today's water-safety methods are ineffective:

"Lifeguards have an impossible job. They sit there for hours in the bright sun, and they're supposed to notice the one kid who's *not* making noise, who's not causing trouble. But how do you notice the unnoticeable? It's counter to everything. We don't notice still and quiet; we notice thrashing and loud, calling out for help."

And parents can't watch their child every second even if they want to: "When they bring them into the E.R. from the public pool, the parents come screaming in after them. And they always look right at me and say, 'I only looked away for a second, and he drowned.'

"I have kids, and, you know…kids sneak away from you all the time. So one kid falls down, skins his knee, starts crying; the other kid slips into the water to play. You're taking care of the kid who's crying, bandaging the knee, while your other child drowns. It doesn't have to happen, though."

By the time a child arrives unconscious at the E.R., Graham can resuscitate some, but some he cannot. For those he cannot, he visits the waiting room to tell the parents he couldn't save their child. He keeps his composure as he talks and answers their questions. But after the event is over, his own tears stream. "I can't talk to a mom whose kid just drowned and not cry. You can't explain this unnecessary death – science can, of course, but I can't."

Graham was deeply frustrated in the face of child drownings, and his helplessness was affecting him badly. He needed a way to release his frustration, so he began work on his electronic "cure" for death by drowning.

People deal with frustration in many different ways: running from it, taking drugs, becoming violent, or hardening their hearts. But some bear down, forcing their frustration into work. For instance, artist Marriott Little objectifies her frustrations in her canvases.

Marriott Little has won over fifty awards in watercolor, oil, pastel, and acrylic on canvas. At her downtown studio in Raleigh, she's blending base colors to find the right shade of blue. Marriott is eighty but has the vibrant energy of a sixteen-year-old and knows how to focus this energy as a force for her work.

She objectifies her fear and anger into art. "You can have all kinds of cares and worries, but if you can create something…your worries are gone. One of the pleasures of painting is that you lose yourself…in a zone of concentrating only on your art."

Marriott adds that creativity and expression are life forces. "In Chinese, they call it 'chi.' For me chi is the vitality of life. It's where the process of creating comes from—the head, through the heart, and out through the hand. It's a life force – an energy for people who want to create. You got to do it, energy comes out. You got to try to do something, you know?"

Yes. One cannot respond to fear, anger, and worry in any better way.

The Rookie Inventor

Growing up in a middle-class neighborhood in Raleigh, Graham liked visiting his neighbor Ed Patterson. Ed invented things for sheer enjoyment. The boy hung around Ed's garage and learned young about lathes and specialty saws.

"Ed's a carpenter, always playing with tools. And he has all kinds of inventions, things he's made but never commercialized. One year at the lake, he starts digging a hole in the beach—probably twelve feet across and three feet deep at the shoreline, so it immediately swamps with water. And then he puts a metal trashcan in the middle, a wood stove in the trashcan, and lights it up. The thing gets hot; it's a hot tub and we're sitting in this sandy hot tub! So my joy of inventing might have come from Ed."

Graham studied chemical engineering in college, finding it interesting. After graduating, he followed his childhood dream of becoming a pediatric physician. But after helping deliver a baby in the hospital parking lot, he changed his mind and in 1999 began practicing emergency medicine.

"Although emergency medicine is heartbreaking, stressful, and intense—emotionally and physically—there's no reward like it," Graham says. "People are broken and often I can get them fixed. In every case, I'm free to follow my heart, regardless of whether the patient has insurance or status. And I don't stop to judge what you were doing that got you into trouble—the only thing is doing my best to make a broken person fixed. That's the greatest moment in all of medicine, assisting at the dramatic focal point of humanity's pain."

Objectifying Frustration into Creation
(Three Years 2005 – 2008)

Singer, songwriter, and winner of twenty Grammies, Bruce Springsteen avenges the working class by transforming their rage and resentment into energetic lyrical music, as in his song "Dancing in the Dark," from the 1984 album *Born in the U.S.A.*:

"Man, I ain't getting nowhere,
I'm just living in a dump like this.

There's something happening somewhere,
Baby, I just know that there is."[49]

Entrepreneurs often follow a similar path as Springsteen—
turning frustration into creation, into making something valuable
that solves their problem and calms them by discharging their intense feelings into the work. For entrepreneurs, that's a product,
service, or idea and the message and effort that sells it.

In 2005 Graham and his Wake Medical Hospital colleague,
Dr. Courtney Mann, Director of the Children's Emergency Department, began collaborating on a plan to reduce the number of
child drownings in their E.R. "Dr. Mann and I were drinking wine,
lamenting the losses of children that we had had in the E.R. from
drownings when she said, 'We should invent something that when
a child gets too deep in the water, it shoots ink into the pool so the
lifeguard can find the kid.'"

"Yes! I have gigabytes of information in my pocket, but I'm
still using the same technology—lifeguards—that they used in
the 1800's to protect my child from drowning?" Graham added.
"What if we set off an alarm?"

His initial research showed that attempts had been made to
invent anti-drowning devices, but none had worked effectively.
He didn't believe, though, that *nothing* could be done about the
heart-wrenching losses. He wondered if a device could sound an
alarm if a child was underwater too long.

So Graham began tinkering in his basement. Often as late as
two or three in the morning while his family slept, Graham tried
to build an "anti-drowning device" that would respond to being
underwater too long. "I didn't know whether it would work or
not. I didn't know whether you could sense water intake to deploy alarms. So I took apart a flood sensor to figure out how that
worked."

For more than eighteen months, he taught himself about circuit board layouts, capacitor timers, CAD software, programming, and other electronics. He needed to learn all that before he could prove to himself that an anti-drowning device could work. He had to see how those systems worked, so he could move forward to solve his own problem: "How can I prevent children's deaths?"

Engineers told Graham that he should pay someone to use a computer to figure it out, but he refused. "I told them, 'I need to understand this at the base level.' And so I did. I learned what's called assembly language. It's not quite programming using 0's and 1's, but it's almost that complicated."

In hindsight Graham admits that eighteen months was a long time to tinker with SEAL. Later though, he didn't consider it wasted time because this hands-on work allowed him to pour his heart into SEAL Innovation and use that emotional commitment to advance the project. He knew that once something becomes an obsession—that's when great things can happen.

Graham was reaching the point that this wasn't just a "business" he was fostering—it was an obsession.

Raising Capital...And Hearing Crickets (2007)

He discovered that an anti-drowning device was possible, but making it 99.99% reliable would require a much greater effort. "The more I looked into it, I saw it's actually a lot more complex than I thought," he said. "Solving that problem in a reliable way that's not like an annoying car alarm that goes off every time you hit a speed bump is difficult."

Isn't that how most projects go? Often, getting 90% to the goal is the easy part, but the last 10% takes the most time, energy, and creativity to solve. "The devil is in the details" fits entrepreneurial creation to the letter.

Graham's basement invention, he saw, was too complicated, too large and heavy, thus too impractical; it worked only part of the time and used out-of-date technology. And he hadn't yet validated that it could one day become a real product nor had he formally interviewed experts or potential buyers. To turn his invention into a product required advanced engineering, trials, and marketing.

He needed capital to pay for all three processes.

In 2007, Graham created an LLC, SEAL Innovation, whose purpose was to invent new products, including the SEAL. He wrote a simple business plan, made a demo video, and beat the bushes contacting roughly twenty angel investors and venture capitalists to get financing.

After eighteen months, only four firms had agreed to hear his pitch. Graham had little success raising money. "I was selling an idea but just didn't get any interest," he said laughing at himself. "I'd make a couple of pitches and maybe three phone calls.... Then they would say, 'Okay,'... And then I would never hear from them again—it was just crickets out there."

He learned from that experience that venture capitalists and most professional angel investors rarely invest in "ideas" per se. They normally invest at a later stage when a good idea has made more progress in terms of research, product completion, market validation, and revenue traction. And they normally invest in businesses with experienced management teams. Graham had none of that.

"Early stage for a venture capital company is a young and accelerating business; not a 'This-might-work!' business," Graham says. "Selling an idea with a plan when you're not well known and don't have a track record is very, very difficult."

I'll Put My Chips In... (2008)

After three years of hard work, he hadn't convinced investors. Undeterred, Graham was confident that his basic design was *technically* possible. However, his prototype was bulky to use to survey possible customers and didn't look like a real product, thus it couldn't fire up investors' imaginations.

Raising money for entrepreneurial ventures can feel a lot like trying to get one's first credit card. You can't get a credit card because you have no credit history. You can't get a credit history because you have no credit card. Yet Graham knew he'd have to move the ball forward to raise money successfully next time around. "There's this crazy standard you have to meet in order to get investment," he observes. "You have to earn investment by showing that the ball's going to advance whether you get investment or not. It's illogical but highly revered and accepted in the game."

Graham decided to double down, invest more of his own money, and pursue the SwimSafe with more gusto than ever.

"I was at highly feisty point where, if the investors didn't do it, fine. I'd put my own chips in. I would just basically do everything . . . short of ending [my] marriage, to advance it," Graham says. "But I accepted taking some real pain, some economic pain, on myself because I was that confident that I was going to succeed." Acceptance of sacrifice, in this start-up game, is as important as obsession and determination.

After that decision to invest his own money, Graham interviewed engineering firms that could work up his SwimSafe invention into a real product. Most firms were too expensive, but he found one with good ideas and paid them $20,000 to improve upon his homemade prototype. Because of his excitement, the decision to spend $20,000 wasn't difficult, but...

"I'm sure you've heard this a million times, but it takes more money and more time to do things than you think. And so, I would have thought, for that $20,000 we'd be done, wrapped up, and off to market. In my naïveté, spending the $20,000 was an easy decision because I thought for $20,000 I'd be getting a final product. Not so!"

The engineering firm worked for several months and made the SwimSafe more reliable and less clunky, but it was nowhere near ready for market. "I didn't quite have 'buyer's remorse,' afterwards, but I thought, 'That's it?' I wanted more. What I saw showed me I wasn't even close to done."

In order to build upon the engineering firm's prototype, again with his own money Graham hired two engineers experienced in working with start-up inventions. They worked for him part-time for a combination of stock options and pay.

This bet paid off because the engineers made good progress. Not only did they build more reliable parts for the SwimSafe, raising the viability percentage above 90%, they also fine-tuned the practicality of how it would work. For example, they showed how the company could offer two products.

The first product monitors *all child swimmers* in a pool. Swimmers would receive a transmitter (worn by the swimmer) when they register at the pool, and lifeguards would then monitor all children from one central location. The monitoring system (the receiver) would keep track of all swimmers from a central location.

The second product, for individual purchase, monitors a *single child or a few* children in a pool. Instead of central monitoring, the receiver is a wristband that the guardian wears to monitor his or her child's safety.

Since Graham had little experience in business and marketing, he also brought on a part-time marketing professional, Lena Cox, who had had sales and marketing positions at IBM and Citysearch. com. Lena helped him focus the features customers desired from an anti-drowning device and developed communication plans to publicize SwimSafe to potential partners, inventors, and customers.

Graham had learned about the importance of patents from devising an earlier invention, so in 2008 he successfully patented his new invention. He saw it as beginner's luck. "I sent [the application] off, and the patent office said, 'Okay. Click! You got it.' Our attorney said, 'Wow! That never happens.' I think what SEAL Innovation received is called a first-action approval. I figured, 'Oh, yeah, I'm good at this.' And so I wrote a bunch of patents. To the new ones, they said, 'Easy, killer.'"

After receiving his initial patent, Graham wondered if a larger firm might want to acquire the product. That way, his idea could get to market much faster on a larger company's infrastructure and experience. So he met with a few suitors to explore their appetite for such an invention.

"We did a lot of traveling to meet with potential customers and acquirers. It was still too early, I realize now. Even so, we were making contacts and seeing if there were people who would want to [acquire us].

"I learned that what most large companies do now when it comes to consumer products is they let another company develop the device, and then they buy the device. And if the young company's already got some channels, sales channels, they buy the whole company.

"A guy who owned a large national safety firm told me, 'We've got a hundred and forty products in the queue. The only way you get moved to the top is if you're already selling. Then, it makes sense for us.' And so...what they said to me was, 'Hey, come to us when you're in sales and we'll talk.'"

So there would be no easy exit. No big sale right after the patent.

Second Attempt at Raising Capital

By 2009, nearly three years into the project, Graham had improved SwimSafe to a degree of reliability and product appearance he liked. So he met with several national swimming organizations and got their blessing that *conceptually* the SwimSafe was a good idea. But they also told him that his prototype needed more work. "They asked me, 'When can we get it?' But they also told me, 'You have problems here, here, and here.'"

His life-saving device wasn't market-ready. "It did the job, but it looked like a medicine bottle swinging from your neck," Graham said. "And it wasn't durable. That was a non-starter right there. It has to be both small and indestructible for pools to rent out to seasons of children."

Improving it to that point would cost more money.

Graham was still going at it alone—at least financially. He had already invested $100,000 of his own cash for engineering, marketing, materials, patents, and travel expense. But up to this point, his costliest investment was sweat equity. "Every time I don't go into work, that's very expensive," Graham noted. "It's tremendous. There will be six-month periods where every single day, I'm never working [for SEAL Innovation] fewer than three hours a day and sometimes putting in ten, eleven hours."

According to Payscale.com, an emergency room physician earns between $92,582 and $363,774 annually.[50] Since Graham practices medicine in a large, busy hospital, he likely earns on the topside of that scale – at least $250,000 – or roughly $130 per hour. Since the beginning of 2007, Graham estimates he's worked on the SwimSafe fifteen hours per week, or about 2,300 hours. That translates to roughly $300,000 in lost income, a significant figure that needs to be taken into account.

To build a marketable product Graham budgeted $350,000

to continue paying his experienced engineers and buy materials, technical drawings, CAD software, research certifications, and marketing. For example, the circuit board for one SwimSafe device is too tiny to assemble by hand, so robotics is required.

He considered two options for raising capital: spend his own money or try a second time to raise it externally. Ideally, he wanted to raise it externally. "There's only so much pressure I can put on the family," he says and also he wants to save his cash in case the company needs money down the road.

Setting out again to raise money externally, he chose to raise it from high-net-worth individuals, not only from venture capitalists.

Initially, in order to practice his argument, he pitched to investors who he didn't think would be a good fit—like practicing with a net. "I selected groups where none of the people were going to be interested. I mainly wanted to get feedback from them." Most presentations took place in his home with a projector, Powerpoint, product videos, and creative props to show the SwimSafe in action. "I've got an aquarium and a hot tub with prototypes, and I set out some chairs," he laughed.

Graham explained to investors that the SwimSafe worked but needed more engineering. "The device was kind of silly-looking, but I could say, 'Hey, watch what happens when this kid goes under. Jrrzzzt! – red alarm! See?' You wouldn't want it on television with consumers looking at it, but a person who has a basic understanding of technology understands, 'Wow, that works. If you shrink that into something that looks slick...'"

Graham pitched fifteen presentations to forty serious investors, but also many more to passive investors. Some investors wanted to hear the same presentation four or five times before they would make a decision.

Aligning investors' values and Graham's mission was the most important partner consideration. "It's very important to me that investors have realistic expectations for the company and its mission. I'm going to want their input. I want people to ask hard questions. I want opinions that I can respect and that are generally in line with mine, but that push my thinking forward."

The fund-raising efforts went well this time around. Most liked his pitch and believed the SwimSafe had a good chance of success. It appeared that Graham's approach of keeping the ball rolling by integrating investor feedback had worked—the SwimSafe now looked like a feasible idea.

During the fall of 2010, SEAL Innovation successfully closed its investment by selling 15 percent of its stock for $365,000—equating to roughly a $2 million valuation. The $365,000 came from fifteen different investors - eleven individuals and four angel investors who had experience investing in start-ups. Most investments averaged about $24,000.

Graham personally invested another $40,000 to maintain majority ownership and voting control of the company and to prove to investors that the price was fair. "I re-upped," he explained. "I invested at that stock price. I felt like, one: I owed it to the investors to say, 'Hey, I'm buying at the same price.' Two: I didn't want to lose majority control. So I had to buy my way back into majority control." Graham would also be Chairman of the newly formed board.

Putting $365,000 to Work (2011)

In exchange for the $365,000 investment, Graham established a goal of providing a product that's workable and nearly ready to manufacture. He purposefully kept corporate overhead low so he could invest most of the money directly into the product. For example, Graham didn't pay himself. "I pay everyone except myself; I don't pay me," he said.

Graham kept several engineers on as contractors and made sure they were as excited as he was to be partners. "Since they got stock options, they give a lot more than subcontractors would because these are my partners."

The team worked on finalizing the SwimSafe's functionalities. "We made drawings, sketches, and tried different formats," Graham said. "What would happen when the kid runs away? What would happen when the kid tears it off? What would happen if the kid smashes it? What would happen when the battery died? What would happen if two kids go down at once? Is it going to have sirens? Is it going to have buzzers? Is it going to have LEDs? All those kinds of things. This is a long process. It's really designing our functional spec."

They also study *how* kids drown so SwimSafe can address commonalities among the cases. "Every single day, I get a little Google alert that another kid drowned," Graham said. "I always want to know the details. I'm looking for common themes and how they happen, so that we can structure the systems to prevent it."

They are improving the device's usefulness, with Graham's eight-year-old son, Jack, as the guinea pig. "I throw [Jack] in a pool or throw him in the lake, and we just play and play and play and play with the SwimSafe."

That work demonstrated that several more technical improvements were required for SwimSafe to become a workable product. For example, they needed extensive engineering to waterproof the device – a much more involved process than engineering it only to be water resistant.

The SwimSafe also must be easy to use. "The goal is to have one button, max," Graham explained. "No battery changes. Do nothing to it. Here it is; put it on and it works. I want it as profoundly simple as possible." They're adding enhancements like a LED light so that if a child is drowning in water with poor visibility—in a lake, for example—he can be located quickly.

Perhaps the most significant improvement has been the engineers' progress in enabling the transmitter on the child's necklace to detect a problem. The original creation relied mostly upon buoyancy—and was therefore not 100% reliable since drowning involves many more conditions than lack of buoyancy. So the engineers created an algorithm that monitors water depth, pressure, wetness, dryness, motion, distance, and other pre-programmed variables that make the device fail-safe, pushing its workability close to 99.99%.

Graham pushes the engineers for fast turnaround, appealing features, and a limited budget. In response, the creation process has required compromise between the engineers and Graham's grand vision. Graham's role has been similar to that of Steve Jobs at Apple—pushing and inspiring his team to create a product that goes beyond what a reasonable businessperson would believe it plausible to design and construct, given SEAL Innovation's limited resources.

According to Walter Isaacson's biography, *Steve Jobs*, Jobs pushed Apple's engineers and design teams to make product features that were apparently impossible.[51] But Jobs would force them to figure out how to make the impossible possible. In a similar manner, Graham pushes his engineers to build the SwimSafe on a fast timeframe, free of errors, despite limited financial resources.

"Our engineer tells me, 'You're trying to squeeze all three sides of the balloon,'" Graham says. "'You're trying to squeeze time, money, and scope. You can't squeeze all three. Something has to give. Sure, if you give me ten years, I can do it. Or, if you give me ten million dollars, I can do it in a week. If you don't care if it leaks, I can do it. But you gotta give me something!'"

But thanks to hard work and ingenuity, in early 2012 SEAL Innovation delivered on its commitment to provide investors a reliable product as small as a pack of gum. Graham remembers fondly the first time the SwimSafe worked without errors.

"We're at the pool doing test number 10,000. As usual, we take out our equipment, monitors, graph paper, and start taking notes. Usually something always goes wrong. But this time when testing it, we checked everything off and I said, 'It worked.'

And then we were like, 'IT WORKED!" HOLY COW. IT WORKED! DO YOU KNOW WHAT THIS MEANS?' I wanted fireworks to go off or something. But instead it was kind of anti-climatic. Well—I guess now we'll move to the next step—manufacturing. But I wanted to take a moment.

"We've done what we set out to accomplish from a moral point of view. We've created a device that saves a child—at least on a one-off basis. Now all my fears that we couldn't do it are gone. Like what if we just couldn't detect drowning? Or what if technology is just not there yet? It is. We've built it. It works. Now we just need to make one every twenty seconds."

Where Is SEAL Innovation Now?

From 2012 until 2015, Graham was focused on perfecting the SwimSafe and building scalable manufacturing processes. Early in 2016, the SwimSafe was released to the public! His recent email to me read: "Madness and mayhem 243657 but loving it."

While early adopters for difficult to find, as with each stage, Graham is overcoming the challenge. He has several YMCAs engaged and implemented. One YMCA Aquatics director says, "We are adding an extra layer of protection for our kids while continuing to train vigilant guards...It's the only swim safety tool I have ever seen that kids actually enjoy using which has been fun to watch."

SEAL Innovation has also raised $2 million from an angel group and is marketing and selling its SwimSafe all over the world.

Creativity Doesn't Guarantee Business Success

Thomas Edison, an inventor who was awarded 1,093 patents, has earned larger-than-life fame through his inventions—the practical lightbulb, the phonograph, and significant inventions used to make movies. Yet when Edison passed away in 1931, his estate was valued at $12 million—a lot then, but not a lot considering how many enormously successful businesses were built upon his inventions—like General Electric.[52] Nor does $12 million look like a lot compared to Henry Ford, who in 1936 with *one product*, the automobile, donated $109 million to endow the Ford Foundation.[53]

Edison's first inventions improved telegraphic transmissions. He could have focused on building up a business around the telegraph, but instead he licensed, partnered, or sold his ideas to keep inventing other products. He didn't take business very seriously. Edison once said, "Invent it, and they will come."[54]

But "Invent it, and they will come" goes only so far. Beating out the competition for limited resources is hard work and a learned skill. In order to do that, most new products require great attention to production efficiencies and marketing effectiveness.

One day SEAL Innovation will likely need a Henry Ford, not just a Thomas Edison. SEAL Innovation's management team will need outstanding execution around management, marketing, and operations. Author and business management guru, Peter Drucker, warns in his book *Innovation and Entrepreneurship*:

"Even when it is based on meticulous analysis, endowed with clear focus, and conscientiously managed, knowledge-based innovation still suffers from unique risks and, worse, an innate unpredictability."[55]

SEAL Innovation's future success is dependent partly upon uncontrollable factors. Consumers are fickle, emotional, and irrational in their buying. Therefore, we can't predict with high certainty whether SwimSafe will appeal to them. After all, one aspect of child drownings that doesn't seem to help demand for Swim-Safe is parent denial that his or her child will be the one to drown on a given summer day.

But SEAL Innovation's future success is also dependent upon *controllable factors*. It will need a full-time leader with a careful business strategy to be successful. Now that Graham's invention works, the focus has shifted away from creativity and more to business matters such as pricing, manufacturing scalability, and relationships with suppliers. SEAL Innovation must convince early adopters to buy SwimSafe. Engaging these early adopters will require hard work, experience, and persuasion.

To date, Graham appears to have a knack both for invention and for management. But for him to manage SEAL Innovation in the future, assuming SwimSafe succeeds, he'll likely have to give up practicing medicine and inventing because the business itself will need great attention to detail and thus absorb all his work hours.

As for who runs the company in the future, Graham is open-minded to doing whatever is best for SEAL. Just because the device was his idea, then his obsession, he doesn't need to run a company—especially a large one.

"Usually there are start-up CEO's, and then there are finished-product CEO's," he explains. "If the production of Swim-Safe has to be done by another CEO, and I have to step away from it for the benefit of the company, then I'm all-good with that.

"What's important is to complete the mission of preventing

drowning; the obligation to the investors; and the success of the business. Do I need to walk around with a CEO title? No, I'm good."

Being its CEO isn't a necessity to Graham. He doesn't want to sit in business meetings; he'd rather go on to solve bigger problems through invention. "Yeah, I don't know if I could keep my passion managing a $100,000,000 business. Maybe I would. But I have so many meetings already, you know? Most times I'd rather be in the lab inventing stuff."

Conclusion

In which creation flows from the head through the heart, then through the hand.

The Walt Disney Company produces films and owns and operates eight theme parks and resorts and dozens of media companies. ABC and ESPN are two of them. In 2011 it produced $41 billion in revenue and had 156,000 employees.

Company founder Walt Disney spent ten years, 1919-1929, trying to turn his idea of producing animated cartoons into a viable company. As an eighteen-year-old go-getter, Disney wanted to make something of himself. He had watched his father, Elias Disney, lead a hardscrabble life while struggling to find career success. Elias bought an orange grove in Florida, but a freeze destroyed his crop. He purchased a farm near the apple pie town of Marceline, Missouri, but his lack of farming experience and falling crop prices resulted in failure. He had to sell the farm, saddening young Walt, who had loved Marceline.[56]

In 1911 the Disney family moved to Kansas City in search of work for Elias. Walt loved to draw and dreamed of one day creating a comic strip. He dropped out of high school and apprenticed to the cartoon department of the *Kansas City Star*.

Walt became fascinated with hand-drawn objects that appear to move on film—a new idea called animation. In response, he built his own small production studio in older brother Roy's garage, and worked there nights and weekends learning the craft. "When he'd come home and long after everybody else was [in] bed," Roy remembers, "Walt was out there still, puttering away, working away, experimenting, trying this and that, drawing, and so on."[57]

At nineteen Walt started his own company that produced one-minute cartoons, "Laugh-O-Grams." For example, one of his films poked fun at Kansas City's slow streetcars by showing daisies growing from a woman's hosiery while she waited for a streetcar. Struggling financially, Walt promoted his humorous, satirical films to theater chains, making a few dollars here and there.

To grow, Laugh-O-Grams purchased animation equipment with a $15,000 investment from Walt and his friends. Disney worked day and night for two years, rarely earning enough profit to pay himself a salary. "We twice had to move during the night because we couldn't pay the rent,"[58] said Rudy Ising, an unpaid high-school student Walt hired as one of his first employees. Another employee said there wasn't enough money to buy "three square meals a day." But even when the chips were down, Walt was optimistic and believed everything would work out in the end. "He had the drive and ambition of ten million men," an employee recalled.[59]

In 1923 Laugh-O-Grams was forced into bankruptcy because the cost to produce the films was more than the amount theaters and distributors paid to show them. But Walt was undeterred and swore to pay everyone back. "Most people filing for bankruptcy are disturbed or bitter," said Walt's attorney who handled the bankruptcy. "Walt wasn't."[60]

Walt moved to Los Angeles to begin a new life so excited it

was as if he "were lit up inside by incandescent lights."[61] He carried with him only a small, frayed cardboard suitcase full of animation equipment.

In Los Angeles, Walt printed new stationary, "Walt Disney Cartoonist" and searched door-to-door for a distributor of his latest animation, *Alice in Wonderland*. While trying to prevent bankruptcy in Kansas City, he had written several distributors soliciting their consideration of *Alice In Wonderland*. One letter went to Margaret Winkler, a leading animation distributor in the country. She and Walt worked out a deal for her distribution of *Alice in Wonderland*, but he couldn't earn a profit. But there was a bright side his hard work, though—his animation quality was improving.

In 1927, Walt finally had some credibility, partly a result of his new character Oswald, a floppy-eared rabbit. Universal Studios contracted with Disney's distributor to buy several copies of Oswald videos. Disney travelled to New York to devise a favorable contract with his distributor, but instead of signing a new deal with Walt, they cut him out by hiring his employees. All of his hard work for nothing!

Walt didn't quit after being betrayed by the distributor. Instead, partly as a reaction to his desperation, he became even more obsessively creative, just as Graham Synder did in 2009. During Disney's train ride back to Los Angeles from New York, he conceptualized a new character—this one a mouse with round ears and a button nose: Mickey.

In Los Angeles, Disney hired a few available ex-employees and set them up in a garage to produce Mickey Mouse's first film, *Plane Crazy*, completely on speculation and with no contract in hand. The film cost Disney $1,772—money he didn't have, so he needed to sell it fast.[62] But he couldn't.

Distributors rejected *Plane Crazy*, yet Disney gambled again—this time adding sound to improve it. "We'll make [it] over with sound. That's it. That's it!" Walt exclaimed.[63] Distributors were concerned that voices coming from animals would be unnatural, but Walt believed it would work.

Finally, after taking out more loans and negotiating with multiple distributors, on November 18, 1928, Mickey Mouse's *Steamboat Willie* debuted as the first animated film with sound effects.[64] The Mickey Mouse animation series grew in popularity, and in 1929 Disney created the Mickey Mouse Club. The club provided stage activities like pie-eating contests and sold Mickey Mouse paraphernalia after Mickey Mouse movie showings.

Mickey Mouse became the catalyst for Walt's success and led to his producing from 1937 to 1967 eighty-seven full-length pictures, including *Snow White and the Seven Dwarfs*, *Peter Pan*, and *Mary Poppins*. Eventually Disney Studios was the entertainment empire it is today.

Walt Disney's story shows the primacy of a belief in one's creation in order to keep risking and fighting to make it viable. Second, an inventor is driven by a simple, child-like curiosity that drives him or her on and on to see what he thought of, then made, out there being used and appreciated by others.

French philosopher and writer Jean-Paul Sartre writes, "I have tried to do the following...to prove that genius is not a gift, but the way out that one invents in desperate cases."[65] Entrepreneurs like Walt Disney and Graham Snyder, no matter how desperate and frustrating their start-up problems are, don't generally run away from them. Instead, they dredge up extra energy and cash to solve the problem before them. A little puzzle inside their heads won't go away; it demands to be solved, to be seen fixed in the world. They objectify frustration, transforming it into creation. Artists turn the same frustration into their crafts—whether music or painting or sculpture.

"I've been called passionate to a fault before...actually, I'd say fairly often," Graham said, laughing. "When I feel strongly about something, I cannot let it go. And that's served me well."

Many important creations often don't happen fast. Bruce Springsteen took six months to record the song "Born to Run" and had to defend the time it took: "Spontaneity is not made by fastness. Elvis, I believe, did like 30 takes of 'Hound Dog.'"[66] Graham has needed ten years so far to produce and market the SwimSafe. Walt Disney needed ten years to make the Walt Disney Company a viable business.

Graham, ten years into his project to save children from drowning, has raised and spent a lot of money, a portion of it his own. But he presses on. Building the SwimSafe has been an iterative undertaking involving several incremental steps:

tinkering for eighteen months in his basement;

failing for eighteen months to raise capital to improve upon his homemade invention;

investing $100,000 of his own money to hire engineers to improve his home-made prototype;

earning a patent on the SwimSafe;

failing to sell SwimSafe to a larger business;

raising $350,000 to make SwimSafe smaller and more reliable; and

working nearly 3 years to get the SwimSafe manufactured in a scalable manner.

Taking the Phases, One by One, Without Being Fazed

Graham threw himself into each of these phases and did his best with limited resources. In fact, he believes investing his long-term sweat equity feeds and motivates the creative process. "I taught myself how to program, how to integrate circuits and how to write an assembly line, which took a colossal number of hours,"

Graham points out. "As soon as I get to a certain point, all that sweat becomes unimportant, though, because I've got somebody else who can manage the project [even better than I could.] "But they never would have been interested if I hadn't made the thing work at all. And so was that wasted time? I don't think it was. And I can apply what I learned there to the next project."

Furthermore, these incremental steps Graham experienced helped him develop an emotional link to his creation. Now SEAL Innovation isn't just a "business"—it is his mental construct in time, his obsession, and a part of his life. And the obsessive approach enables him to press on and continue to innovate. That's the creative, dynamic loop that fuels eventual success.

The 2008 Panel Study of Entrepreneurship II (PSED II), a joint effort among leading researchers to gain insight into how companies are created, interviewed 1,214 engaged in a start-up. The second survey, twelve to eighteen months later, showed that many of the start-ups hadn't yet entered the business-related phase one might expect. For example, only 39% of them had opened a bank account, 18% had hired a lawyer, 13% had received outside funding, and 10% had signed an equity agreement.[67]

What were these entrepreneurs doing during those twelve to eighteen months? According to the survey, 79% of them were investing their own money in the venture, 76% of them were talking with potential customers, and 65% were creating product models or prototypes.[68] They were often still tinkering with their idea, just as Graham explored circuit board layouts in his basement while his family slept. Or, as Walt Disney learned the basics of animation in his brother's garage.

Tinkering is a hands-on, trial-and-error process of exploring product possibilities. Tinkering provides the clues to move the idea forward. For example, Graham was unsure of the SEAL Innovation's viability when he started. "I didn't know whether it would work or not," Graham said. "I didn't know whether you could sense water intake electronically. So I took apart a flood sensor to figure out how that worked." Likewise, in the beginning Walt Disney produced one-minute cartoons called "Laugh-O-Grams" that didn't earn him much money but taught him about animation.

Like artists, entrepreneurs tinker, using Marriott Little's "chi"—energy stemming from the head, through the heart, to the hand. "Chi" was Graham's energy source for creating the Swim-Safe. The frustrations he felt at seeing healthy children dying in his arms swirled in his head, the images taking a toll. When his frustration became heart-felt, Graham collaborated with colleagues to take action—turning his concern into even greater energy-giving force. That energy flew to his hand when he started tinkering in the basement late at night to create a tiny, wearable anti-drowning device for children.

"Chi" is not unique to Graham. Just about every entrepreneur leverages this energy source to create as well. Walt Disney was frustrated by his father's unsuccessful ventures and turned that emotion into creation. Frustration for entrepreneurs comes from many different places. The desire for independence, the desire to solve a heart-wrenching problem, or a need to make the world a better place are but three of the energy sources for starting an innovative business.

Entrepreneurs and artists create in a similar manner. Like an artist, Graham and Walt didn't create their businesses in a rational, organized manner, having to meet specific deadlines, checklists, and other structures. Instead, the innovator eats the elephant one spoonful at a time. Invention is a work of art, full of failures, tweaks, good ideas, bad ideas, blind alleys, and hard knocks—before the moment in which it all comes together.

For entrepreneurs who enjoy creating new ideas, and can come through the above risks, handling the business matters of their start-up may be a personal sacrifice. Negotiating business strategies, especially as the start-up grows, become paramount to its success. Business and art integrate for successful entrepreneurship to continue past viability. Especially if the founder didn't pursue his idea primarily for economic reasons, he or she finds it grueling and oppressive to have to adapt to market conditions.

Yet one of the most beautiful aspects of entrepreneurship is its flexibility to adapt to the founder's desires and temperament. For example, part of the reason that Graham is eager to get the Swim-Safe into production is to find time to invent more helpful products.

"I do feel like time is slipping away...all the time..." Graham says. "My biggest incentive for getting [SEAL] flying forward is that I feel pent-up with wanting to develop the next project. The product line that we're expanding focuses on child and personal safety and monitoring.

"For me [starting businesses] is mostly about solving problems. The desire to find new solutions to problems is what drives a whole lot of what I do. I compare the abundant resources we have in the United States with the entrenched problems we have, and see that some of that doesn't match. There are so many problems we can't or won't solve, but there are some that we can. That's where I want to be."

Whether SEAL Innovation succeeds or fails financially, then, isn't Graham's biggest concern. That concern is to help prevent children from drowning. "If you didn't make millions of dollars off it, is that a failure? No, it's not," Graham explains. "You advance the ball for someone else. Of course, I'd rather advance it for me and for my investors. But I'm just saying that it's not at all wasted if it helps save children's lives."

Advancing the ball—that is the overall dynamic of entrepreneurship. But within that, creation flows again and again from the head through the heart, then through the hand.

Chapter 6
My Own Start-up, First Research:
Building a Viable Company with Limited Capital

A start-up's hockey stick blade-length measures the time period in which a founder advances a good idea to its growth inflection point. In order to get to that turn, some founders raise capital, then race to market to gain market share before other entrepreneurs discover the same idea. Other founders are patient,  choosing to "bootstrap" in order to save money, maintain greater control of the new company, and slowly figure out the most productive work processes as their company grows.

Introduction

First Research sells industry reports for salespeople written in a concise, easy-to-digest format. I thought of the idea when I was a young banker making sales calls to businesses whose industries I didn't know much about. Without knowing that business's larger context, I couldn't suggest concrete ways the bank could help the customer solve his or her particular problems.

For example, I was meeting with the owner of a retail furniture company who had two store locations and was considering opening a third. "I'm trying to figure out if I'm going to buy my next store location or lease it," he said.

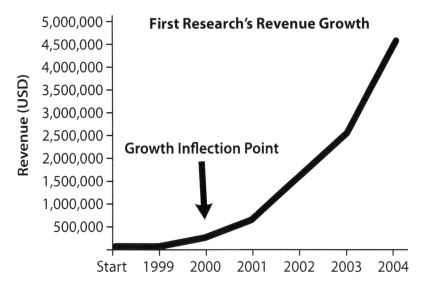

Ideally, as his banker, I'd have some financial advice for him. But I had little knowledge about the furniture retailing field, either its genesis, history, strengths or problems today, or what it might be doing in the future. I'd have to ask him a host of basic questions just to get up to speed. He'd feel I was a newbie wasting his time. I left that meeting thinking, "It sure would have been better if I had had the basic information about the retail furniture industry upfront." Not knowing really robbed me of the authority I need to sell him relevant financial products.

In response to similar unproductive meetings, I created a new type of clear, concise online industry report useful to busy sales and marketing people, accountants, bankers, and other customer-facing professionals. First Research Industry Profiles are like Cliff's Notes for industries—each profile has 10-15 pages of background education, industry trends, financial statistics, and links to additional information.

I started First Research in 1999 with business researcher Ingo Winzer. We grew it from $4,000 in revenue our first year in business to $6.5 million in 2006. In 2007 we sold First Research to Dun & Bradstreet, the leading provider of business information, where it has since continued to thrive.

First Research was a classic bootstrap start-up business—built with sweat equity and about $30,000 in seed capital. Instead of seeking outside capital, we reinvested most of our revenue in growth strategies.

Bootstrapping and the Wild West

Like many idioms in the English language, the term "bootstrapping" evolved from folklore, then from written stories. In Rudolf Erich Raspe's 1781 book, *The Surprising Adventures of Baron Munchausen*, the Baron sinks to the bottom of a swamp and when all hope for his survival is lost, he uses his own strength and inventiveness to pull himself out of the muddy water by his own hair.[69] The story is a tall tale, but the hero's far-fetched success mirrors the human desire to survive and thrive. It's an adventure, but also a narrative of hope, betterment, and will to succeed against all odds.

Early in the nineteenth century, beating back America's frontier inspired another version of Raspe's story—wherein a man pulls himself over a fence by his bootstraps. The notion of using extraordinary self-determination to succeed spread with books such as Horatio Alger's *Ragged Dick* (1868).[70]

In the early and mid-1800s, trappers, mountain men, and gold miners who explored the western frontier represented the "bootstrapping" mentality—venturing into the wild with nothing but the bare necessities. They relied upon their personal ingenuity to survive in the wilderness while carving out financial rewards and a better way of life. Legendary frontiersman Christopher "Kit" Carson ran away from home in Missouri at sixteen and headed west—fending off Apache Indian attacks, wild animals, and harsh weather in the Rocky Mountains before he succeeded.

Robert M. Utley's book, *A Life Wild and Perilous*, shows how frontiersmen like Carson sought independence and adventure. "The mountain men did not head west for selfless patriotic motives...hey went to make money in a pursuit that promised adventure, excitement, personal freedom, and the nearly total absence of authoritarian restraint."[71]

Bootstrapping entrepreneurs are modern-day frontiersmen—seeking unfettered adventure by using their personal skills to survive on their own. Like Kit Carson running away from the comfort of his Missouri home, entrepreneurs often leave the security of a cushy corporate job to work on their own project—not knowing what's ahead and relying upon rugged individualism to survive.

Bootstrapping a start-up company means starting a business with few financial resources. Today, the hazardous frontier does not concern fighting with wild Apaches, but the risks of defying conventional capitalism. Without money, you are a greenhorn, a fall guy. So a bootstrapped start-up leverages the founder's creativity, ingenuity, practicality, time, sweat, and cost-cutting ideas to make it go. Some of these ideas include bartering; taking little or no salary; issuing stock instead of salary as employee compensation; obtaining financing from credit card companies, friends, and family; working in garages or second bedrooms; and taking odd jobs to pay bills.

Bootstrapping entrepreneurs wear many hats, completing tasks themselves that big companies often hire professionals to do. They design their own marketing brochures, draft their own customer agreements, devise their own bookkeeping systems, and sell door-to-door without sales experience.

Such a haphazard approach to earning a living makes entrepreneurship seem risky—leaving a great deal to chance. And to cap it all off, bootstrapping usually means working for little or no pay, sometimes for two years or more, many times with a growing family to support.

With all these unpredictable factors out there, starting an innovative company may seem like venturing into the wild.

(Not So) Quiet Desperation

In our middle-class suburban neighborhood in Raleigh, North Carolina, my father was a mathematics professor and my mother was a middle school English teacher-turned-homemaker. When I was ten, my father bought a farm where I helped him build fences, clear brush, grow crops, and tend cattle. I peddled strawberries and asparagus door-to-door in our neighborhood, cut grass, and held other odd jobs to make spending money. But sports was my thing—pickup football, basketball, soccer—or whatever was in season.

Throughout most of grade school I was a lousy student. My lack of maturity and short attention span led to my "repeating" fourth grade. I was hyperactive, and if I were a kid today, doctors would put me on Ritilin.

But in high school my history teacher Don Goodwin noted and encouraged my entrepreneurial interests. Mr. Goodwin was tall and lanky, a confident outsider with charisma who humorously mocked sports events, proms, cheerleaders, spring break, student government, and pop culture.

Yet Mr. Goodwin was independent in a productive way, instilling in me a sense of optimism and confidence that one can be different and still be relevant in a conventional setting. No need to be a conformist if you didn't want to.

Mr. Goodwin's inspiration also helped me improve academically, and in 1993 after graduating from university, I started my first job, working for NationsBank (now Bank of America). I dreamed of becoming CEO and pioneering industry changes, but after a few years I realized that my chances of living that dream were doubtful. To succeed in banking, maintaining a cool political-correctness was paramount. But that reserve didn't come natural to me.

I was frustrated hearing the barrage of platitudes common to large companies: "We empower our employees to make the decisions that are best for our customers." Fine, but in practice we salespeople are told what to do and how to do it.

While venting to my Uncle Brian, a retired corporate executive, about the B.S. at the bank, he said, "Remember, Bobby, your job is to implement policy, not create it." Brian's terse words revealed that my dilemma was unsolvable. Towing the line would have to be my M.O. for the next 40 years! My career had hardly begun, and I felt like a failure, and claustrophobic.

Like western frontiersmen, I wanted "adventure, excitement, personal freedom, and the nearly total absence of authoritarian restraint." I didn't want corporate execs limiting the creativity and power I could bring to my sales job. But most of all—I wanted to amount to something and not feel like a failure in my career.

Turns out many entrepreneurs are motivated by fear of failure. Manfred E.R. Kets de Vries, author, co-author, or editor of more than thirty books and 300 papers analyzing aspects of entrepreneurship, writes in his article "The Dark Side of Entrepreneurship":

Some entrepreneurs I have known hear an inner voice that tells them they will never amount to anything. But regardless of who put this idea into their minds, these people are not retiring types who take such rebuke passively; they are the defiant ones who deal with it creatively through action. They possess enough inner strength to prove the voice wrong and show the world that they amount to something (163).[72]

That was me. One of my primary motivations in starting First Research was to amount to something.

But how and where could I start a company that would amount to something and reflect well upon me? And what would it be about? The obvious answer was to start a business that was innovative, one in which I could take skills I didn't have out of the equation but use and stress the skills I did have.

An Idea Morphs
(1995 - 1997)

I needed a good idea. I had toyed around with starting businesses like selling soccer apparel or performing services for banks. But at the time, those ideas didn't appear profitable. Now I wanted an idea that would enable me to fulfill my desire to amount to something.

The idea that became First Research was a nexus of clues embedded in experiences I had while working at NationsBank. In addition to feeling underprepared to help the retail furniture owner make financial decisions, other moments of truth gathered force, impelling me to break away from the bank.

In 1995 Sam Catlett, a business officer with a competitor, was the best bank salesman in town. When my boss asked our customer, president of a steel company, what made Sam an effective salesman, he paused, thought for a second, and said, "He's smart, asks good questions, and knows a lot about steel." I thought, "True! How can I compete with that?"

But if I wanted to compete using knowledge to my advantage,

how would a 25-year-old banker like me learn anything relevant about steel—its history and present situation? At the time, in 1995 he could request information from NationsBank's industry research department, whose purpose was to collect industry information for the bank's employees. To get industry research prior to calling on a large restaurant chain, I'd had to submit a form by fax a week in advance. I'd received a package via interoffice mail of about 50 pages of poorly unified material that I myself had to analyze and gather into some sort of usable order. It was a painstaking, inefficient learning process.

When I received the restaurant industry information, I went through the material page by page looking for content relevant to my customer's situation. When I discovered information that could help me, I'd hand-write notes that would ultimately lead to questions I'd ask the prospective customer on a sales call. After I made my notes and saw the value of those sheets in prepping me for sales calls, I wanted to improve upon them.

My handwritten "cheat sheets" were the genesis of First Research profiles.

Without thinking, I took my idea of creating industry "cheat sheets" straight to the manager of NationsBank's industry research department and suggested he provide them to the rest of the bank. He rejected my idea—"costs, time allocation, technology, timing, and capabilities" – the usual corporate bull. I spent the next twenty minutes trying to show him why he was wrong, why better material would increase sales enough to more than offset his department's costs, time, and so forth.

But my efforts were a lost cause, so I began to consider starting this business myself. After all, I wanted good, organized, concise cheat sheets, yet they weren't available to any salesperson without great difficulty and lots of lead-time before a customer meeting. I could solve that nexus of nerve-wracking sales problems.

Kicking the Tires
(1997 – 1999)

In mid-1997 I set out to start a "sales-friendly industry report for salespersons" business while still employed by the bank. Because of my own need for the reports, I believed I had a good idea, something salesmen needed beyond a doubt.

Was I qualified to start an innovative business? I had never started or run a business. I had never managed one person. I had little money. I hadn't taken any classes on starting a business. I hadn't read one book on how to start a business.

But none of those practical hurdles ever once crossed my mind. In fact, I believed I was smarter than I actually was. Looking back on it now, I see I was a greenhorn wandering off into the mountains without a knife, matches, or a full canteen.

To start my business, I needed a partner who could write industry reports. I never considered raising money from an investor because this was before the dot.com era. The first person I contacted was a woman who worked in my bank's industry research department. When I met with her about my idea, she said there was no money to be made by selling research. With a cocky grin she kept repeating, "You gotta eat!"

After that rendezvous with the industry-research associate, I kicked the can down the road for several months, but I also tinkered with my idea. I'd go weeks without doing much of anything on it—figuring that there was probably more than an ounce of truth to what that industry research manager had told me.

Sometime in early 1998 I finally completed a business plan that explained my idea and offered financial projections. I proposed a 50/50 ownership split with any willing, qualified partner. My business plan looked like a sophomore term paper: typed on copier paper; printed on a low-quality ink-jet printer; set in a white three-ring, drugstore notebook, using dividers cut from paper and glued to tabs.

To find a partner I approached large research providers with big-name brands. For eighteen months beginning in 1997, I mailed my business plan to six large research companies, including Dun & Bradstreet, Frost & Sullivan, and Freedonia. The vetting process at those big companies was slow-moving, and none in the end took my idea seriously.

Two Guys with Nothing in their Hands (1999)

Occasionally a blind squirrel finds a nut because it searches so long. By late 1998 I downgraded to pursuing smaller, niche research companies as partners. One potential partner that turned me down was Stax Research, headquartered in Boston. Since he was turning down my idea, its CEO, Rafi Musher, wrote three names on the back of a napkin during our lunch together.

One name was Ingo Winzer. I thought, "Ingo Winzer? Interesting name." Ingo was a self-employed real estate analysis guru whose second-bedroom company was called Local Market Monitor. Ingo's ideas were often quoted in *Barron's, The Wall Street Journal, CNN,* and other media. He had credibility, so I contacted him:

Ingo: "I can create a research product, but I can't sell."

Bobby: "I can sell, but I can't create a research product."

The first time I met Ingo in January of 1999 he was to pick me up at a street corner in Boston. He arrived twenty minutes late in an unwashed, gray Toyota Camry. I figured he'd be big-city serious and formal, but he wasn't at all like that. With light-brown hair falling slightly below his shirt collar, he wore black jeans, a gray T-shirt, and cowboy boots. I wore pressed khakis and a blue sports coat. Here was an intimidated, small-town Southern banker flirting with a super-intelligent, laid-back Yankee cowboy to start a company.

Under his disparate regional style, though, Ingo Winzer had wisdom, humility, and sincerity—coordinated by a brilliant mind. Ingo took just a day to design a nifty, efficient process for creating industry reports. His accompanying email said only, "Voilà!" I was amazed—and hooked. That attached report was just what young bank salesman Bobby Martin had needed five years before—and never gotten. And Ingo added quality and consistency to my cheat sheet – making the product appear professional. Ingo Winzer had solved my own business problem.

Next, Ingo and I devised a back-of-the-napkin ownership and organization structure. I would quit my bank job and become president. Ingo would keep his Boston-area business, Local Market Monitor, spending half his time on that and half on my research company. I would finance the start-up expenses. Ingo would write the industry reports for no compensation. I would own 65 percent of the business and Ingo 35 percent. As for future compensation, Ingo suggested, "How about for every $2 you pay yourself, you pay me $1?" He had a knack for keeping things informal and simple, yet logical. That was our handshake "deal" for the first year until we signed a shareholder agreement that formalized the same structure.

So on a cold, blustery day in early March of 1999 I called Ingo from a cell phone outside my Wilmington, N.C., bank office. "Are you in?"

"Yes!" he said. Two minutes later I walked back inside, resigned from the bank, and never looked back.

These first few months starting the company brought to light for me eighteenth-century poet, Thomas Gray's observation: "Where ignorance is bliss, 'tis folly to be wise."[73] I was clueless, yet years later I often craved again the youthful innocence of that time. Being on my own was a time of bliss, exuberance—bouncing so high partly as a reaction to my new freedom from depressing corporate shackles.

I had quit my "real" job to start this fragile but needed company. Ingo and I had plenty of unanswered questions: Would anybody buy our research reports? If so, how much would they pay for them? Were banks our best target market? I hadn't completed market studies. I had asked very few bankers if they thought it would work. It was just a hunch. We didn't even have a name.

And Ingo and I had committed to each other without answering important partner-related questions. It was like a couple meeting at a bar and eloping to South Carolina the next day. How long was each of us committed to the venture? If we were successful, what would we do with the profits? Were we creating a "growth" business that adds employees or a "lifestyle" business that remains a simple structure with very few employees? What provisions would be included in our shareholder agreement? We didn't discuss any of that stuff. We just hustled to the altar and got married.

As Ingo recalls, "We didn't sign our shareholder agreement until the end of the first year because we didn't know if we had a business. First Research was my first experience of starting something from scratch, from two guys with nothing in their hands," Ingo said. "Now I know that this is how you *can* start a business—with nothing."

First Research didn't *exactly* begin with "nothing"—rather, with just a little. To finance the start-up, I cashed my former employer's employee stock-option plan, netting me about $12,000. Start-up expenses included $5,000 for a password-protected website; $500 for web publishing software; $1,500 for a computer; $1,000 for professional editing; and $1,500 for a brochure and logo.

Our biggest investment would be sweat equity – working without pay. Our monthly budget, which well-funded start-ups call a "burn rate," was a mere $2,265 per month – mostly my personal living expenses. For example, my mortgage payment was $465. Ingo's living expenses were covered by his existing business, Local Market Monitor. Since First Research had no revenue, to fund my personal losses I borrowed $25,000 using a handful of family stocks as collateral. Plan B was that if I ran out of money, I would work in a restaurant at night.

In the beginning we had no product, so while Ingo was writing research reports, I kept myself busy by helping him and overseeing our website design with a local web service firm, Orotech, in a strip mall wedged between a strip-club supply store and a pizza joint.

I named our company First Research—a name a friend and I dreamed up one evening over beers. A small local marketing firm helped me create an upside-down Nike swoosh below *First Research* as the logo we kept until 2004.

Lousy Sales
(June 1999-March 2000)

By June 1999 we had a limited product based on Ingo's report prototype, but I was ready to land our first batch of customers. My sales strategy wasn't sophisticated—I called banks and asked them to buy the product. To figure out what to charge for a subscription, I asked myself, "How much would I pay personally for access to something like this?" I settled on charging $200 per banker per year, or about half a *WSJ* subscription fee.

Despite the sparse conditions, I was confident that First Research would take off. My business plan forecast that in the first year we would land 207 bank customers and generate $907,000 in revenue. "The timing is perfect to bring this product to market," I wrote. "The window is wide open due to a number of key factors, including: 1. The definite demand for the product coupled with a lack of competition..."

To reel in my first batch of customers, I hired my girlfriend's roommate to mail prospective customers, most of them banks headquartered in North Carolina, a sample industry report and cover letter. Not one bank called me back. Surely, as soon as bankers saw my brilliant idea, they would be amazed, stand in awe, and rush to get their hands on it, right?

So I called them. A few bankers vaguely remembered receiving my mailer. Several bankers hung up. My day-planner from August 17, 1999, shows I had called thirty-one people, almost all bankers, and left twenty-eight voicemail messages, designated "vm." That classic sales project failed miserably.

Next, I tried leveraging "warm" introductions. A friend's father, a lawyer for banks, introduced me to several bank presidents he knew. I met with a few of them in person to show them my idea. The bank presidents didn't say "No" and they didn't say "Yes"— instead they jerked me around like a rag doll.

About half of the bankers rejected my idea. A redheaded, fifty-something, overweight loan executive at a tiny South Carolina bank lectured me in a slow drawl, "Baaa-beh, I don' understand what yah doin' hee-ah. How long have you been doin' this? I jes hate to see a young man like yah-self wastin' so much time with this silleh thaaang. Baaa-beh, we ARE the bank – we already DO this!" Because this guy had gotten personal, I remember his words and tone like my first kiss.

I also tried to get in the door at big banks. After spending several weeks fact-gathering on Wachovia Bank, I figured out that the right contact was Sheryl Struthers, who had a strategic role in how its bankers sold to businesses. I mailed her a letter requesting a meeting and included lots of detail about First Research. She ignored my follow-up calls for about two months and eventually mailed back a corporate-MBA-speak letter reeking of arrogance.

Not every prospect engagement was terrible, though. Bradley Thompson, president of SouthTrust's North Carolina Bank, connected with our value proposition immediately. In a seersucker suit on a hot day in September, he paced his conference room hypothesizing why First Research's reports could be valuable. Months later he became our first customer, signing a $6,250 contract, but for now, he just liked what he saw.

Even so, after six months of pitching First Research to banks, I was becoming desperate. I needed some quick wins to pay my personal bills. One of my gambits was to sell First Research reports for cheap to anyone who might need them—high schools, university libraries, business schools, research departments of any kind, and investors. No luck there, with the exception of one $500 subscription to a young man starting a consulting firm.

I figured that economic developers might need industry reports to help them learn about businesses they were enticing to move to the area. I pitched, they waffled. But they offered me $1,000 to complete an ad-hoc research project gathering facts about companies considering moving to the area. I needed the money so I took the deal. Earning those first dollars made me feel the most alive I'd ever been in my career – as if I were living in the woods and surviving neatly on my own.

On a fall day in 1999 I bumped into an acquaintance – an accountant. In telling him about First Research, he asked if we had a report on Food Distributors, so I gave it to him. He liked the report so much that he referred me to an association of accountants.

The accounting association's leader was impressed with our product and promoted us to her members. The results shocked me – and we landed about twenty small accounting firms at $599 each.

First Research was in business – sort of.

For the next several months that success gave me an evangelistic shoe-salesman mentality and I refocused again on banks. I preached the gospel of "call-preparation research" to anyone who would listen. To pitch prospective banks, I created presentation booklets about First Research: background, pricing, value proposition, and so forth. Each booklet was custom-made—I was proud of the color pages, tabs, and the prospect's logo on the front page.

I bound them at Kinko's, telling their employees, "These are really important!"

Then I blew my tiny marketing budget on 500 blue and gray mouse pads with our logo and tagline, "Accurate Industry Data Fast." Giving prospects those booklets and mouse pads felt like I was handing them two passes to the Masters.

Despite the few highs, we struggled during that first year and the results were disappointing. A rational investor might conclude that on paper First Research was failing. Year-end 1999 we had $399 in cash, $899 in accounts receivable, and a $20,150 loan payable to me. Revenue was just shy of $4,000—compared to the $907,000 I'd predicted in my business plan.

All-in on a Pair of Sixes
(2000-2001)

Early 2000 was a turning point for First Research because I could feel the pendulum swinging in a positive direction – not because customers were finally buying – they barely were. But by then, I was giving First Research away for free to select bankers and they liked it. One email said: "I'm using First Research – loved it. I called on the president of a trucking company and didn't know much about it, but after reading your report on it, we were conversing about diesel fuel prices like I was an expert…."

Emails like this were more inspiring to me than taking on a new customer.

Ingo recalls that enthusiasm was our best asset. "After a year we still didn't know if we had a business. That didn't matter to me. By then I was pretty confident something good would happen, mainly because you were so excited about what we were doing. I think every new business needs that, infectious enthusiasm. Just having a good idea isn't enough."

By February 2000, I was beginning to land a few accounts with banks – $750 here, $1,500 there. For the first time, I could smell victory for First Research.

What I did next was one of the gutsiest career moves I've ever made. Before we had consistent income or money in the bank, I hired a salesman. I had my man picked out well in advance—Wil Brawley, a kind-hearted 20-something just a few years out of college. He had worked with me at NationsBank – where he sold deposit products to businesses. The guy would show up at work with tousled hair and a disheveled suit, then charm those around him with personality, wit, and energy.

From the very beginning, I wanted Wil to join First Research. During the summer of 1999, I had begged him to join us as a salesman—offering him 20 percent of First Research's stock and 50 percent sales commission with no base salary. But he declined because he was moving to Los Angeles with his fiancée and needed consistent income. No matter: I kept recruiting him whenever he would listen. I didn't know any salesperson better than Wil so I recruited no one else.

By March of 2000 First Research had a trickle of small customers – maybe two or three per month. But most importantly, by giving away the product in the form of pilots, I had built a pipeline of prospective customers, including a large one that I believed would eventually buy our product. I called Wil and begged, "We need you,

Wil! We have customers now – like real customers. And I might be signing a $40,000 one. We can even pay you base salary."

Again, Wil declined my offer, but twenty-four hours later, after a bad day in his own bank job, he accepted. "I need $4,000 a month to survive. If you can make that happen – I'm in!"

In March 2000, one year after Ingo and I had started First Research, Wil joined our adventure. We gave him 10 percent of First Research's stock, a $4,000 salary, and 20 percent commission. Committing $4,000 a month was risky, like going "all in" with a pair of sixes in a poker game. I had spent most of my personal funds and sales were coming in haphazardly. But so what? Now was my chance – so we moved $4,000 per month in chips to the center of the table.

By mid-2000 I began making sales while Wil got up to speed and built a pipeline. Despite his sales ability, though, Wil didn't close new sales immediately. Selling First Research was like acting out Samuel Beckett's *Waiting for Godot* [74] —we'd wait and wait and wait. Long sales cycles were a way of life for us.

But 2000 was still the year of promise. We earned $227,000 in revenue – and most of that came in the second half. I paid myself $11,200 in salary, plus I repaid the roughly $30,000 I'd loaned First Research for start-up expenses. Most of that year's revenue was invested in writing more industry reports and in paying Wil's base salary.

Innovative start-ups hit a growth inflection point when they discover methods that can be duplicated. At that point, success becomes the process of *repeating* successes. The founders are no longer bootstrapping, asking themselves "Is this idea viable?" and "What can I do personally to get customers to pay my personal bills?" but instead: "How can I *repeat* this effective process faster and better?" In essence, Wil and I were each shifting from trial and error to scalable, standard methodologies.

Three Guys and a Dog
(2001)

In 2001 First Research became more innovative. A big part of my job was now prioritizing our smatterings of feedback into product improvements. We added more frequent industry updates, additional financial data, email alerts, and training. We didn't charge customers additional fees for those improvements, but chose to expend more effort finding new customers.

Mostly we continued to invest in our cold-call selling-machine. Early in 2001, we plundered Bank of America again, which would become a trend, and hired Lee Demby. Lee was hard-working like Wil and me, but he was more of a thinker, a planner—very thoughtful in his approach. We offered him stock in First Research and made him the same income package as Wil's. Wil and Lee lived in Charlotte, 150 miles from our "world headquarters" on the coast in Wilmington. Wil and Lee focused strictly on selling to banks, while I explored selling to new markets, one of which was outsourcing companies like ADP.

Wil, Lee, and I sold hard then, our sales method based upon our personalities, experiences, and biases. We were folksy, down-home, jovial, hands-on, scrappy, and open. For example, some start-ups try to appear bigger than they are, but we thrived on being the underdog.

An executive once told Wil, "I'm sorry for asking so many questions. I'm just trying to make sure you aren't two guys and a dog." Wil paused. "Actually, we're *three* guys and a dog. Our president, Bobby, has a dog." The man laughed, shaking his head and grinning. He may have seen Wil as genuine and fresh. Liking Wil, he easily came to believe in him. The man's company became a customer shortly thereafter.

Selling with Wil and Lee in 2001 was for me the best of times for First Research. We treated it like our own game of Survival. "Each prospective customer was like a new game of chess," Wil recalls. "Some of them left the king, the decision-maker, exposed relatively quickly. But most made you work hard to get to that king. I knew we'd win every single game if we stuck with it long enough. People saw it in our eyes and heard it in our voices. We sold a great new product with fire, passion, energy, enthusiasm, confidence, love, and honesty. We were genuine. Our product was unique."

And our cold-calling machine was paying off. In 2001 First Research earned $726,000 in revenue, and my salary grew to $74,700. We used the revenue that year to beef up our savings account, hire Lee, and add more product enhancements.

Calibrating the Machine
(2002 - 2004)

Wil and Lee taught us that cold calling was a profitable exercise if we were patient and persistent, learning from each incremental error we made, each abandoned rabbit hole we fell into. That lesson transformed First Research from a tiny, second-bedroom operation into a real business. First Research would no longer be about hand-to-mouth survival—it was now about finding more "Wils and Lees."

Revenue increased to $1.6 million, $2.5 million, and $4.3 million in 2002, 2003, and 2004, respectively. We plowed that cash into a two-pronged strategy: hire more "Ingo's" to write more industry profiles, and hire more "Wils and Lees" to sell them.

"Wil and Lee" were becoming more than just two people—their approach to selling had become a cult philosophy for me—I was a believer! I rarely used their names separately. Together they were both a noun and a verb. "WWW&LD – What would Wil&Lee

do?" "You need to Wil&Lee it to succeed!" It was "Wil&Lee this" and "Wil&Lee" that.

I hired people who'd drink the Wil&Lee-flavored Kool-Aid: Susan, Darren, Debian, Gretchen, Carolyn, and others. They'd drink it or be damned! My "Wil&Lee" sales strategy did work well, too.

At that time, First Research was still a flat organization with about a dozen employees. But the employees were lone wolves – each did his or her own thing based on relatively broad mandates created by the team—not just targets "sent down" from me. Our business didn't have much complexity to it at that time, and today I look back on the period as our "The Wonder Years," a 1990s sitcom about the age of youthful innocence.

My most challenging work was teaching new salesmen the "Wil&Lee Cult" selling method and helping them cope with long sales cycles. But beyond that, I just made small tweaks and improvements to our productive sales methods. It was like calibrating a machine – give it a little more gas, but don't choke it out, tweaking just a little here and there so the machine ran smoothly.

Growth Comes With a Cost
(2005 - 2007)

During 2005 and 2006, First Research grew to over $6 Million in revenue and had more than forty employees. We were growing fast, diversifying our customer base by selling into new markets like technology, outsourcing, and insurance. One of my original motivations was to make something of myself, so the fact that First Research was growing felt good. Growing felt like an addiction – and I thrived on finding out what was around the next corner.

But as we grew larger, I also discovered that bootstrapping

techniques that had helped us survive weren't as scalable now. For example, entrepreneurial direct-selling methods were becoming more difficult to duplicate. Part of the reason that Wil&Lee poured their hearts into selling First Research was that they were shareholders and felt part of building something new. A customer once told Wil, "You sell through force of personality. But that's not something that can be replicated" in a large sales staff.

That observation applied to First Research—I had begun to notice the same challenge. I'd have to find new selling methods that we could replicate as a larger company. For example, I wanted to figure out how to sell more small subscriptions to millions of small businesses. That sales approach, however, requires different skills – like marketing and process management.

The result? In targeting new types of customers, as well as targeting many more customers, we became less entrepreneurial and more corporate. Growth has a way of doing that, of forcing leaders to organize and standardize methods, wringing some "personality" and individualism out of the business process because they are too "slow," too non-standard. Sad but true. And so the cult philosophy "Wil&Lee" was not only becoming less practical, it was less popular among the new hires in the First Research office, too. To find new methods, I hired some smart people with diverse ideas who wanted to try new things.

My growth strategy wasn't overly popular with Ingo, Wil and Lee, though. I added new managers like Tyler Rullman, a 30-something Harvard graduate with an M.B.A. from UCLA who had good ideas about how to grow. He advocated First Research "professionalize" each department by hiring experienced managers in each practice area: sales & marketing, product, technology, research, and finance. I supported Tyler's idea. First Research was changing from being "naïve, energetic, and entrepreneurial" into a full-fledged company with five stable departments, budgets, vice-president roles, and a modern office with cubicles, conference rooms, and a kitchen.

After Tyler and the other corporate-type managers were added to the growing team, Ingo noticed his and Wil's roles being marginalized. "It was clear to me that Tyler quickly became your biggest influence, a role that Wil and I had shared before," Ingo recounted. "This wasn't a bad thing because Tyler is a smart guy, but both Wil and I felt marginalized. When you and Tyler started hiring a research department, I was on my own. And Wil was not happy with the shifting roles you and Tyler assigned to him. No complaints, I'm just pointing out the [naturally] shifting influences as a company grows."

Growth had come with a cost.

I felt caught in the middle relative to how fast we should grow. Ingo, Wil, and Lee felt that First Research was changing too fast, but the managers I had recently hired felt that we weren't changing fast enough. They thought I was being too conservative since First Research maintained good profit margins, had a large cash reserve, and never considered raising capital. And they also didn't like that I questioned spending money on strategies I didn't fully understand, like running expensive marketing campaigns to attract more customers.

While First Research was becoming a larger organization, I evidently appeared to be a satisfied leader. Dede Houston, who joined First Research's marketing department in 2005, told me, "You were passionate, driven, and positive—a very infectious leader, Bobby. The sky was the limit and we were all going to succeed. If you were sweating, you never let us see it."

Despite First Research's necessary growth into a cooler, more corporate identity, I still considered it my baby. But it needed to go to off to college and live free of daddy's control. I especially had difficulty letting go of our folksy, down-home selling methods.

Those selling methods were as much mine as were my boyhood memories of throwing a ball around in the yard with my dad. It became more challenging to protect my comfortable methods as we grew and had to integrate new ideas. I couldn't, and sometimes wouldn't let "traditions" go. That was a problem.

Those closest to me were aware of my dilemma. Carolyn Beggs, who joined First Research in 2001 and became our controller, someone in whom I confided for several years, said: "Most people would classify you as a passionate leader and visionary, but probably not one fully aware of the challenges of running a business. You had sleepless nights worrying about the best decision in all sorts of situations."

My challenges in trying to lead a bigger company were solved on a summer day in 2006 at a trade event in Boston. There I met Mary Bowes, a salesperson with Hoover's. Hoover's, a division of $1.75 billion, is a fast-growth, internet information business. After a two-minute conversation with me, Mary exclaimed, "We should buy you!"

A few weeks later, business development leaders from D&B contacted us to consider "opportunities to work together." I knew those conversations might mark the beginning of the end. First Research was a synergistic fit for D&B and other information companies. But I had never developed an exit strategy, a plan of how one day to sell First Research. Why would I want to sell my baby and call it an "exit?" Cold word, "exit." Close to "abandonment," and that *wasn't* good.

But as Peter Pan says, "To die would be an awfully big adventure."[75]

After several weeks of meeting in conference rooms and over steak dinners, D&B made First Research an offer. After negotiations, on March 20, 2007, D&B acquired First Research for $22.5 million in cash plus $4 million in incentives. First Research has prospered from joining D&B and remains the leading provider of industry intelligence for sales professionals.

Conclusion
In which pulling oneself over a fence using his bootstraps isn't as farfetched as it seems.

EDS, now called HP Enterprise Services, is a multi-billion-dollar information technology company started by former presidential candidate Ross Perot. He came up with the idea as a young man while selling computers for IBM. Perot saw that IBM and its competitors sold *computer hardware* to businesses, but what he knew customers really wanted was a *technology solution* created for their specific needs, including having the right software, custom programming, services, and support. Perot took his good idea straight to IBM's management, but they rejected it. IBM wanted to focus on the hardware business—not on services.

In 1962, Perot, as a one-man operation, started Electronic Data Systems (EDS) with a $1,000 investment. "Starting EDS was months of terror," recalls Perot, "because we didn't have any money. And we didn't know what we were doing."[76]

When he started the company at the age of thirty-two, Perot wasn't exactly sure how he'd turn his idea into a real business, so he searched for workarounds. For example, EDS needed computers in order have a product, but it had no money to buy any. Acting as a broker to solve this problem, Perot looked for companies with unused computer capacity that might sell their excess capacity to companies in the market for it. EDS would support that company's computers by installing the right software, programming them, and supporting them. With this plan, he wouldn't have to lay out much cash to start the business. He'd hire the required employees only when he received a contract.

Perot convinced his former customer Southwestern Life to allow him to sell their model 7070 IBM computers' excess capacity. But when he tried to find a buyer for it, he couldn't find a business to buy it. "After making 77 sales calls, I had not sold a single minute of time on the 7070. The clock was ticking, and I was running out of money,"[77] Perot said. He worked part-time for Blue Cross, helping in their computer department, and his wife, Margot, taught school to make ends meet.

Perot finally found a buyer in desperate need of capacity for 7070 computers, Collins Radio, to process their data. Perot had another big challenge—he had no engineers to fulfill the project. What did he do next? He hired two of the smartest systems engineers he knew, Cecil Walters and Dick Beck, who agreed to moonlight at night to help him pull off the project. "When the project was completed, Collins Radio complimented us on our outstanding staff, service, and support," Perot said. "The facts were that we had no staff, service, or support—just Cecil Walters and Dick Beck."

EDS earned $100,000 from Collins Radio and went ahead from there. Perot invested most of the $100,000 profit to hire another salesman, Tom Marquez, who also worked at IBM. Perot recalls that Marquez was "short on experience, but a natural and talented salesman." [78]

Marquez said that EDS had a simple business model in the beginning. "Things were pretty simple then. All we did was go out and sell."[79]

EDS sold two more contracts that were critical to growth. "With the contracts," Perot said, "we had reached a 'critical mass' that allowed the company to grow and make a profit."

Once Marquez became successful, Perot hired another salesperson like Marquez from IBM. And another. And then another. In tandem with hiring salespeople, he hired systems engineers who could deliver the product. Perot interviewed every single candidate and controlled all aspects of EDS himself.

In 1965 EDS started growing fast when it designed a system for processing Medicare and Medicaid insurance claims. It went public in 1969 – and grew into a multi-billion-dollar company.

Most good ideas like EDS and First Research don't begin as professional, well-financed businesses. Instead, they often start out as bootstrapped operations until the start-up becomes viable.

Using a bootstrapping mentality to start a company might appear unsophisticated, but it's a good strategy to launch an innovative entrepreneurial business. The founder is able to understand incrementally the viability of his or her idea, controlling the inner workings as they develop; identify the nuances that will enable it to grow; and keep his or her ownership interest in the business without making a large financial investment or having to spend valuable time raising outside investment.

First Research and EDS's stories illustrate several characteristics common to start-ups that bootstrap.

The first bootstrapping characteristic is creative survival techniques – using personal ingenuity to make ends meet until the business matures. Perot worked part-time for Blue Cross Blue Shield and his wife worked as a teacher. When he finally landed a contract with Collins Radio, he had no employees. Perot scrambled, hiring two part-time moonlighters to make the deal work.

I also survived by doing things I never did again after First Research finally matured – like doing side research projects for economic developers and selling cut-rate subscriptions. At first, "How much ya' got?" was my pricing strategy. For example, when I started First Research, I'd invest two days and drive 300 miles to close a $500 subscription that I should have sold for $5,000. Three years after starting First Research, I wouldn't have driven 100 miles for a $5,000 contract – much less a $500 contract.

But the economics and priorities at the time required low prices. During that time I asked myself, "How can I sell $2,000 worth of subscriptions this month in order to cover my personal bills?" Five years later I was asking myself, "How can we sell $100,000 in new subscriptions this month plus renew $200,000 in existing subscriptions?" Both questions were posed for nearly the same product, but my business needs were widely different in the two phases of growth.

The second bootstrapping characteristic is the importance of trial and error. Ironically, coming to grips with one's own ignorance is what makes innovative businesses succeed. Perot and I both admit freely that in the beginning we didn't know what we were doing.

Perot made 77 cold calls before finding a business desperate enough to pay him for the computer capacity he was offering. I also wasted a lot of time exploring markets that never went anywhere. And when I partnered with Ingo Winzer, I did so with many unanswered questions. We had no shareholder agreement or formal arrangement – we were just two guys with a good idea. We both went with our gut instincts, making up and implementing formal agreements as we went along. Our partnership could have been a disaster if we hadn't gotten along, but we did get along, so our necessary risk-taking turned out well.

The third bootstrapping characteristic is discovering and replicating personal strengths. Perot was a gifted salesman – once meeting his annual quota by the end of January. He relied on his gift, spending most of his time in the beginning selling his idea to potential customers and employees. As soon as Perot landed his first contract, he started hiring more salespersons to duplicate and refine what he had already learned.

Like Perot, cold calling and direct selling were my personal strengths. I partnered with Ingo to complement my weakness –

research. Whenever First Research could afford it, we hired sales-people who matched my strengths and allowed them to duplicate what I learned. Later on – cold calling and direct selling became a hallmark of First Research, and we used those skills to scale future growth.

Selling isn't the only strength that can be duplicated to grow a company – other innovative start-ups succeed by emphasizing marketing, product expertise, management experience, or capital fundraising. The key is to find the right intersection of skills among your team that matches well the business idea and revenue goal.

For example, 27-year-old Jay Parr also started an innovative business on a small budget out of his home. But instead of making sales calls from his second bedroom like Ross Perot did and I did, he experimented in his tiny apartment kitchen making energy bars. Jay invented a tasty, healthy "meal replacement" bar that today is sold in hundreds of coffee shops, grocery stores, and outdoors stores.

When I visited Jay recently at his Boone Bar manufacturing facility; I found him in the kitchen in his apron and hairnet. He wasn't cold-calling during his start-up phase, though. Instead, he was in the kitchen on the phone bargaining for a better price on pistachios. He hung up, then turned to me: "Bobby, taste a new health bar I'm concocting. This one is banana, cocoa powder, sun-flower seeds, and a little guava nectar." It sold me!

Jay focuses his entrepreneurial energy on what he's good at—creating better and better products through his recipes. His rec-ipe creativity is the "entrepreneurial spirit" and thus the highest strength Jay brings to Boone Bars as it advances from an idea he tinkers with in his apartment to the viable, growing business that it is today.

Is Bootstrapping like Settling the Wild West?

Before frontiersmen like Kit Carson moved into the West, was the West really wild? Luther Standing Bear, an Indian author, answers that question in his 1933 book, *Land of the Spotted Eagle*:

We did not think of the great open plains, the beautiful rolling hills, and the winding streams with tangled growth, as "wild." Only to the white man was "nature" a "wilderness" and only to him was the land "infested" with "wild" animals and "savage" people. To us it was tame. Earth was bountiful and we were surrounded with the blessing of the Great Mystery. Not until the hairy man from the east came and with brutal frenzy heaped injustices upon us and the families we loved was it "wild" for us. When the very animals of the forest began fleeing from his approach, then it was the "Wild West" began.[80]

Luther Standing Bear regards the American West as bountiful and tame, a period when people and nature were in balance. Not until the white man invaded did the West become "wild"—untamed, rough, and hazardous.

Likewise, many believe starting a new business by bootstrapping is "wild"—a scary and risky proposition—where one can get hurt and go to bed hungry from its unpredictable revenue stream. And this isn't a baseless fear for aspiring entrepreneurs to have—just look at the typical challenges a start-up confronts during the first few years:

Revenue is tiny, erratic, and normally inadequate to pay the founders a salary.

Customers and markets are difficult to identify and educate, and therefore selling to each with a clear value proposition is challenging.

A new product often isn't ready to sell when the founder expects to because it needs feedback from real customers before the kinks are worked out, yet setting up a practical customer interface can be difficult.

There are few professionals performing critical tasks such as marketing, product development, and sales. Founders must do many tasks themselves without prior experience.

The new business rarely enjoys organized and predictable systems in critical functions such as customer service.

Fixing each of these typical challenges requires lots of time. Living through such an unpredictable situation may appear "wild" when we're used to monthly paychecks, 401-k plans, health insurance, and an organized day.

But for me, bootstrapping to start First Research didn't feel wild or hazardous. Actually, 1999 to 2001 was the best time of my life because I was surviving by means of my own ingenuity. Despite having little or no paycheck for two years, I had confidence everything would somehow work out. Also, my primary needs were met: I had a roof over my head and food on the table. What else did I *really* need?

First Research also provided what was for me a beautiful gift—a problem-solving creation I had started from scratch. The process of building a business made me feel alive—perhaps close to what Luther Bear describes his people enjoyed: "Earth was bountiful and we were surrounded with the blessing of the Great Mystery."[81]

Like the Wild West, First Research only became wild when we started growing, hiring lots of people who fell into conflict and otherwise disrupted the natural flow of using personal ingenuity to survive. For me, growth ruined what was already beautiful—those necessary decisions and experiences of bootstrapping, like designing our own brochures and going to Kinko's to order presentation booklets.

Starting First Research wasn't as difficult as pulling myself over a fence using my bootstraps. Nor was it as wild and danger-ous as the Wild West is said to have been.

Rather, it was as easy as prioritizing what was most important and doing that first, checking these "to-do" items off a list, one by one. First, it was survival. Next, it was learning from experienc-es through trial and error. Next, it was repeating the things that worked and dropping the things that didn't. Next, the hardest of all—learning how to let go of things that worked in order to make room for even newer, potentially more scalable ideas on a clear course to growth and wealth.

Chapter 7
Bob Young's Red Hat Software:
Bringing Forth Luck—Or Is It Skill?

Most start-ups sell niche ideas that compete in relatively small markets. But a few start-ups develop *big ideas* that shake up huge markets. To survive their beginning years and hit a growth inflection point, big ideas require the right timing, the right people, and the right product. And contemplating the source  of game-changing, breakthrough ideas makes us ask whether success is based on luck? Or on skill? On both? Or on something else?

Introduction

Software company Red Hat supports a particular kind of high-demand open-source software, Linux, that runs servers and other applications. In 2016, Red Hat returned more than $2 billion dollars of revenue, though its unique business model stipulates giving its product away for free. How does that work? Red Hat earns revenue by providing service, support, and official documentation for its software—not by selling the software itself.

Linux is also unique because a customer can easily fine-tune it to a particular need. For example, Cornell University's Institute for Biotechnology and Life Science Technologies installed Red Hat's Linux in 2010 to help it manage data-intensive research projects like DNA sequencing. Financial firm CME Group installed Red Hat to help its trade platform sort and otherwise manage its billions of financial transactions per year.

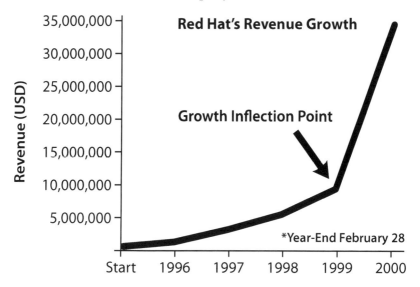

Red Hat's is a David vs. Goliath story. In 1995 when Bob Young and Marc Ewing merged to form Red Hat in a tiny office in Durham, North Carolina, they were taking on Microsoft right in its wheelhouse—software that runs computers: operating systems. In doing so, Red Hat surfed a monster wave and never fell off. How were such energy, strength, and balance possible?

At 60, Bob Young has a boyish face, small, rectangular glasses, and a medium build. He grew up in Hamilton, Ontario, Canada—giving him a disarming Canadian accent. He's earned hundreds of millions, if not billions of dollars, owns his favorite football team, the Hamilton Tiger Cats, and today is CEO of another start-up, Lulu, a self-publishing business. Despite all his success, Bob is personable, down-to-earth, self-deprecating, and even modest. *MacLean's Magazine* profiled Bob as an "overgrown Boy Scout."[82] The perfect description.

Writing about Bob at a local coffee shop, I ran into an acquaintance. I told him I was writing Bob's story of starting Red Hat, and his response was, "Oh, Bob Young. Talk about a guy in the right place at the right time! You know what they say, 'It's better to be lucky than good.'"

Was Red Hat's success the product of luck? Or did something else contribute, too? Something repeatable—that translates to our own ventures?

Riding the Waves

Ten-time world surfing champion Kelly Slater appreciates the role of luck in surfing big waves. His book *For the Love* profiles well-trained and well-prepared friends who have died surfing. Mark Foo, a professional surfer, drowned surfing a wave that should have been harmless for someone of his ability. Experts believe that Mark died after his board leash got tangled in the rocks below. According to *Surfer Magazine*, Todd Chesser, another professional, was killed when a "huge cleanup set pushing 25 feet mowed over [him]."[83] A "cleanup set" is a group of very large waves that break farther from the shore than normal, and therefore, "clean up" a line of surfers caught out there, relaxed and not expecting breakers.

Slater says it was unthinkable that those skilled surfers could die as they did. "Mark Foo and Todd Chesser were both impressive physical specimens who didn't look like they could get hurt. So you just never know."[84] Riding waves is dangerous and disaster can roll over you fast, when you least expect joy of the day to turn on you.

In business, innovation often seems to emerge like a sudden big wave, too. The Gutenberg press, the dynamo, the automobile, and the Internet are all examples of important innovations that inspired thousands of other ideas – sub-innovations. And sub-innovations of sub-innovations appear, too, in certain conditions. For example, consider how many new applications have been built for Apple's iPhone, yet the iPhone itself is a sub-innovation of wireless technology. Sub-innovations develop out from, then latch themselves back onto, the bigger innovation. In a way, sub-innovations surf the wave of the bigger innovation. But riding waves begot of innovation waves can be dangerous and unpredictable.

A Very Bad Student

Hamilton, Ontario, is a harbor town of 500,000 bordering Lake Ontario southwest of Toronto. Bob credits his entrepreneurialism to his being near the bottom of his class there—grade school through college.

"I attribute my entrepreneurialism to my education. I was a very bad student. I think I have a certain degree of ADD. And the joke I make is that had there been Ritalin when I was a kid, I, too, could have gone to Harvard. But there wasn't Ritalin. So I just ended up in the bottom third of my class all the way from kindergarten through university.

"My dad says all the most successful entrepreneurial people he grew up with came out of the bottom of his class. Because those guys learn from experience that the world doesn't work for them. If they can't play the game competitively and beat those smarter than them, their only way to win is to become entrepreneurs and change the world so that it *does* work for them, you know?"

In 1976 Bob graduated from the University of Toronto and

was at a loss for how to begin his career. Bob and his father, David Young, bought a small typewriter-leasing business, Hamilton Leasing and Sales. The business performed well financially, and they sold it to his family's larger business, Hamilton Group. Here's how Bob summarizes family dynamics in the context of running a business: "When it's going well, a family business is no better place to work. But conversely, when it's going badly, there's no worse place to work. That's a long, shaggy-dog story worthy of a whole 'nother book."

This uncomfortable experience awakened Bob's entrepreneurial yen—he clearly needed to be his own boss.

In 1981 Bob married Nancy Beal, and between 1984 and 1988 they had three daughters. He also started his own computer-leasing business, Vernon Sales and Leasing. In 1990 Bob sold it to Greyvest Capital when the Canadian economy weakened. The stock-swap transaction made Bob a millionaire—at least on paper. But soon after the merger, Greyvest ran into financial trouble of its own and its share price tumbled from four dollars to ten cents—reducing Bob's millions to pennies.

At least he still had a job.

Telling Jokes in "C"

In 1991 the Youngs moved to Connecticut to open a Greyvest office in New York City. With personal computer (PC) prices falling, Bob started leasing servers—central computers that run multiple desktop terminals, print drivers, and other applications. To find customers, Bob crashed meetings where programmers talked about the latest trends in the software program UNIX that runs on servers.

Bob's attending these UNIX meetings was instrumental to the later creation of Red Hat. There he picked up the first puzzle pieces that one day he'd fit together to start Red Hat. But for now, Bob was an awkward outsider.

"They had no interest in having sales guys hang out at their meetings," he remembers. "I could pick up from their body language and from a lack of enthusiasm towards me that they had very little interest in my stories. But when they told jokes with punch lines like '/dev/null,' that would bring down the house. We were from two different worlds."

But soon Bob finagled acceptance by offering something the brainy group lacked—marketing and organizational skills. He started a newsletter for them, *New York Unix* that announced meetings and organized user-group sessions.

In 1992 Grayvest laid Bob off, leaving him nearly broke. *New York Unix* was Bob's only business idea at the time, so he incorporated it as ACC Corporation and tried to turn it into a revenue-producing business by selling advertising. He developed a close relationship with his scientist-niche readership, and sought their advice. "I'd ask the user groups, 'What do you want me to write about in this newsletter that you can't get from other publications?'"

Readers kept telling Bob about "free software" and how mainstream computer publications rarely wrote about it. And readers also referenced an obscure free software program called Linux that seemed to be growing in popularity. At the time, Bob had no idea what "free software" or "Linux" were.

The Rise of Linux Software

This software is "free," but not because it doesn't cost money. Instead, the software's source code can be viewed freely and manipulated to do specific work for programmers. Source code is software's building blocks – like the letters of the alphabet or the standard parts that make up a machine. Most software companies, like Microsoft, deem its source code proprietary intellectual property. But free software's code is freely owned by the general public.[85]

Free Software was a movement begun by computer hackers frustrated when companies started claiming rights on code created collaboratively. They were especially angry when, in 1979, AT&T claimed copyrights on UNIX. Programmers weren't happy about that because they had helped create it. They claimed that source code should be "free," meaning available like the alphabet—especially since they helped build it.

Throughout the 1980s programmers embarked upon a movement centered on one question, "Can we build collaboratively a version of UNIX ourselves?" But the collaborative efforts to build a better operating system lacked a key element, a "unifying kernel." The kernel is part of the core software that enables computers to link and multi-task. But in 1991 while working on a personal project, 21-year-old Finnish student, Linus Torvalds, invented a unifying kernel. The unifying kernel led to Linus's invention of the UNIX operating system. Months later he released it under a GPL (General Public License) and called it "Linux."

Programmers combined Torvald's Linux kernel with existing GPL code and the entire operating system became known as Linux.

After that, most Linux development was done under the radar. The only people who took it seriously were geeks and computer whizzes. They collaborated to solve each other's problems, just as university professors collaborate on their sciences research.

Proprietary software companies like Microsoft and IBM also attempted to build operating systems to compete with UNIX. But their operating systems didn't offer user-control, nor did these systems have features attractive to programmers who appreciated free software. At that point, a door was left wide open for a new idea.

The Guy with the Red Hat

In 1992, when Bob was first discovering Linux through his *New York Unix* readership, he assumed the programmers working on Linux were setting up a big corporation to take advantage of their work. He didn't believe that collaborative, altruistic models work effectively to deploy sophisticated technology. "Corporations need a wringable neck," Bob reasons. "They need to know there's an 800 number standing behind their bright kids who are deploying this stuff.

"So I just knew in '92 when I first saw this stuff that IBM, Microsoft, UNIX or one of the commercial vendors was going to take over this opportunity. I thought that it was a fun little experiment. Let these guys have their fun! But I knew they were just setting up the market for Microsoft to be successful."

To Bob's surprise, though, in 1993 Linux's popularity grew while large technology companies continued to ignore it. In response to this growing popularity, Bob published *The Linux Journal*. But his newsletters weren't paying the bills for his family. "My publishing empire was not going well," Bob said. The family was living "on the knife's edge," using credit cards to pay bills. To earn more money, ACC evolved into an online catalog reseller of software applications for UNIX and Linux, books, and other computer-related products. Bob noticed that Linux applications were some of ACC's bestselling products.

So he started asking customers for leads to find more Linux resellers. One referral was Marc Ewing, a 23-year-old Carnegie Mellon computer science graduate with a "scraggly beard and a dirty t-shirt," Bob remembers. Marc had recently started Red Hat, a tiny Linux shop in Durham, North Carolina.

"I had a couple of customers who said, 'Hey, you should talk to this kid who's doing Red Hat, because I got a beta of his CD and it's actually pretty clever. He's going in the right direction.'"

Red Hat got its name from Marc's infatuation with his grandfather's red lacrosse hat. While at Carnegie Mellon, Marc was known for his computer mastery and for being "the guy with the red hat" he wore between classes.

Marc created Red Hat Software in 1994 by accident while working on another software project. His program needed to run on a UNIX workstation, but he didn't have the $10,000 to buy one. Then he stumbled upon Torvalds' Linux as a free alternative to UNIX. Gradually he dropped his first project and started spending his time making Linux easier to use.

"I discovered that I wasn't spending any time working on my project, I was spending all my time fixing Linux and getting it updated and making it easier for me to use," Marc explained in a 1999 interview with Salon.com. "I dropped my other project and started [fixing Linux] as a business."[86]

Marc created a Linux distribution that was more organized and easier to use than the GPL version. On July 29, 1994, he sent a select group his "Red Hat Linux" software loaded onto a red CD-ROM with accompanying documentation and instructions. His version of Linux was well received, getting good feedback.

ACC's online catalog became Red Hat's exclusive distributor. But as separate companies, they struggled in jointly managing channels to market, customer support, and pricing. Within two months of becoming partners, Bob and Marc realized they should be one company.

The Light Bulb Flickers

Since Bob's personal finances were on life support, before getting into even deeper debt with Red Hat, he wanted to learn more about Linux. "I needed to double-down," Bob said. "Before I gambled my kids' college education on this, I needed a little more confidence that free software had a future. So that's when I did this tour."

Bob's "tour" took him to several Linux experts for answers: Why didn't Linux programmers patent and sell their code? Why hadn't technology firms capitalized on Linux?

One stop was the Goddard Space Flight Laboratory in Greenbelt, Maryland, a NASA research facility that was installing Linux. This tour stop was both enlightening for Bob and also instrumental in his creating Red Hat's unique business model.

Goddard was making a big commitment to Linux—replacing a $5 million supercomputer they had bought three years earlier with $40,000 worth of PC hardware running Linux. Bob visited there with a programmer who was writing new Linux code for Ethernet drivers. His plan was to use the new code at Goddard, but also upload it for free, public consumption. Bob wanted to understand why. "You're spending real money on building these sophisticated Ethernet drivers. Why don't you sell them?" Bob asked Tom Sterling, the programmer's manager.

"Because in return for giving away our Ethernet driver code, we get a complete operating system with source code under a license that allows me to put it on as many machines as I can get my hands on—all for free," Tom explained.

"Why are you building supercomputers that run on Linux? I know Sun Microsystems would be happy to give you source code if you would do this on Sun units."

"Yeah, but if I do it on Sun, I have to get my lawyers involved to find out what I'm allowed to do and what I'm not allowed to do with their source code. If I use Linux, I get it with a license that allows me to do whatever I want!'"

Tom had just given Bob a valuable piece of the puzzle—*control* was users' hot button, not features.

"So, what he was articulating was that he was not using Linux because it was better, faster, or cheaper technology," Bob said. "He was using Linux because it gave him control over the technology. And he had no alternative—not from IBM, not from Microsoft, not from Sun, not from Apple—no commercial vendor would give him that benefit. I'm a sales guy. I don't sell features. I sell benefits. And he had just articulated a benefit that no one was willing to deliver—control. So by then, the light bulb was flickering, if you like."

In 1994 Linux was still an under-the-radar, barely-talked-about solution for managing a computer's operating system. Proprietary software firms were ignoring Linux as still being in R&D, so big software firms saw either few possibilities in or threats from Linux. But Linux was quietly gaining momentum, with shipments increasing to 1.5 million units in 1995 from only 100,000 in 1993.[87]

And yet almost no money was exchanged for these shipments, just sharing among computer programmers—like a technology-centered socialism. "When I asked them where this free software was coming from, they would use lines like, 'You know, it's from engineers according to their skill, to engineers according to their need.' Right out of Karl Marx," Bob recalls.

Merging ACC Corp with Red Hat (January, 1995)

Bob's tour inspired him to take the leap and merge ACC Corp with Red Hat. They needed each other's skills—Marc's program-

ming and Bob's marketing. Negotiating merger terms was pain-
less because neither Bob nor Marc thought their businesses were
particularly valuable. They split ownership in the new company
fifty-fifty, retaining the name Red Hat.

Red Hat started as a small lifestyle business, merging personal
and business funds. "The beauty of really early-stage companies
is you know where every dollar is going," Bob says. "So whether I
used this money to pay my mortgage one month, or to buy Marc a
new server, or to pay for Marc's and Lisa's spring holiday—it was
all one pot of money."

To finance the growing expenses associated with marketing
and improving Red Hat Software, they raised seed money from
eight friends and family who bought between ten and fifteen percent of Red Hat's stock. Bob calls their investment "love money":
investing without expectations.

"A love-money round is precisely what it says—people are
investing in your business not because they know anything about
your business, or because they think you're clever. They're investing because they love you."

Suffice it to say, Red Hat's "love-money" investment turned
out to be a good one. In 2000, when Bob's aunt, Joyce Young,
donated $40 million to the Hamilton Community Foundation, that
was the second-largest community foundation donation in Canadian history. Regarding her investment in Red Hat, she told *The
Hamilton Spectator*, "It was exactly like buying a lottery ticket.
You don't expect to win...."[88]

Red Hat's Unconventional Business Model

Red Hat's business model took shape between 1995 and 1999.
"The business morphed. It evolved," Bob said. Its model was
predicated upon an unconventional idea – giving away its product

and source code for free. Bob did that to keep the Linux communi-ty satisfied—after all, they were building his product and he didn't have to pay them.

"It was a small community in the early days, so we knew ev-eryone," Bob says. "Though free software was frequently painted as an ideology or a cultural thing, we approached it as a custom-er-service thing. Our best customers were saying, 'I really want to see you guys succeed. But guys, if you layer proprietary software on it, I can't use your stuff; I'll build my own. So if you just share your code with me as quickly as you can, I'll use Red Hat rather than making my own.'"

Red Hat gave customers what they wanted by effectively horse-trading with them. Customers took advantage of Red Hat's pre-assembled version without paying – source code and all. And Red Hat also benefitted from analyzing the enhancements and contributions customers made to Linux without paying for the privilege.

Red Hat's business model was different from other Linux start-ups. Competitors' management came mostly from the software in-dustry, so they did what they knew, and built *proprietary* software applications that ran on Linux. For example, Caldera Corporation created a Linux Network system with proprietary features that they sold.

Red Hat's idea, on the other hand, was unique in giving away its product for free. But how would it make any money? The an-swer became the genius of Red Hat's business model, the ener-gy-point that allowed it to stay balanced on the crest of a huge wave going forward.

To figure out Red Hat's business model, Bob also spent a great deal of energy learning from those *who didn't adopt Linux*, another kind of tour for him. He discovered Linux was often too complex for non-adopters. For example, more than 600 separate

185

programs make up Linux. Who on the customer's staff would maintain them all, and who would keep track of each one's updates and changes?

And Linux non-adopters perceived that programs were maintained by long-haired programmers in far away places—not ideal for running mission-critical company functions. Companies were used to having support, security, confidence, and backup plans direct from their software providers. They wanted "official" documentation to show their bosses and auditors that they had a legal right to use the programs. Linux didn't offer any of that. It appeared to lack support and reliability. Therefore, Linux wasn't widely adopted. Only computer scientists in back-office cubicles in organizations like NASA installed Linux in 1995.

What if Red Hat somehow responded to the non-adopters' objections? Would they then adopt Linux? But how could Red Hat sell a product that addressed the needs of Linux non-adopters without alienating the Linux community?

Red Hat began distributing the same product two different ways:

a free, downloadable version that included the software and source code

a CD-Rom "official" version that customers could purchase.

Both versions were the exact same software program – source code and all. The key difference was that Red Hat's "official" version included a product serial number, installation guides, how-to manuals, customer service, and support. To its buyers, the Red Hat Linux paid version stood solidly between hackers and the establishment.[89] Buyers regarded serial numbers and support as insurance against loss.

And because Red Hat hadn't had to invest the man-hours to build Linux, it could compete aggressively on price. Red Hat Linux, therefore, retailed for $49.95, compared to Microsoft's Windows NT's retail price of between $150 and $314 or more.

So control over software was the key benefit of Linux that proprietary software makers Microsoft or Sun Microsystems or UNIX couldn't provide.

Bob credits that strategy as Red Hat's greatest decision. "Our biggest single thing was [that] by abstracting away from all the noise, we understood that the core benefit the users were getting from Linux was not better, faster, or cheaper software. It was control over the software. And by being committed to delivering that value to our customer, control, we avoided a lot of the mistakes of our competitors."

Bob succeeded by working with the industry's flow, not setting his energy against it in a defensive posture.

The Wave Begins to Form:
Learning to Attract Paying Customers
(1995 – 1996)

In 1995, Red Hat's first year in business, it recorded $930,000 in revenue and lost $155,000. Most of its revenue that year didn't even come from selling Red Hat Linux, but from ACC's catalog sales of software, books, and applications. Red Hat Linux was barely getting started—it was then still based upon Marc and Bob's grand vision.

But Red Hat Linux's popularity was growing among computer engineers, most of whom downloaded its free version. Red Hat released upgraded versions of its Linux software with memorable names like Picasso (May, 1996) and Colgate (October, 1996). Newer versions installed useful applications like advanced editors, email routers, file transfer protocols, network controls, databases, and Web servers.

Red Hat's paid-version sales slow-cooked. In 1996 most people didn't know how to use Linux. "From '95 through 2000, everyone conceived the value of it, but very few people actually understood how to make it work," Bob recalls.

In the beginning, most of Red Hat Linux's limited sales came directly from computer programmers calling the 800-number or ordering on its website. With such a low price point, $49.95, Red Hat needed greater sales volume, so Bob looked for other places to sell Red Hat Linux. "We're talking two years; it slowly got into more and more distribution channels," Bob says.

To grow, Red Hat needed to be in retail stores like CompUSA. But to do that, they'd need a distributor. Ingram Micro, one of the world's largest software distributors, at first declined to carry Red Hat Linux—fearing a small start-up might leave them with stale, unsold inventory. Since Bob was persistent with Ingram for more than a year, they finally agreed to carry Red Hat. His diligent follow-up paid off because by 1998 Ingram and another distributor accounted for 54% of Red Hat's sales.

Red Hat's eventual revenue growth would derive from getting large sales, installing Linux on thousands of servers for corporations. But from 1995 to 1999, executives at large corporations resisted Red Hat Linux because they still thought it was unreliable. "All of their engineers who liked Linux said, 'Oh, my boss is such a pointy-haired idiot!'" Bob says.

The "pointy-haired idiots," a *Dilbert* cartoon metaphor, were the technology directors, high-level executives responsible for technology at big companies. Bob's conversations with them usually followed the same script, with their declining even to advance conversations.

For example, at the 1996 UNIX Expo, Bob explained the benefits of Red Hat Linux to a giant financial firm's technology director and then asked, "Can I interest you in buying a hundred copies of Linux from me?"

The technology director declined, telling him Red Hat would never fly at his company. "What you're telling me about Linux is you guys down at Red Hat – and you admit there's only fifty of you working away in the tobacco fields of North Carolina – by your own admission are writing maybe five percent of the code that I would buy on your disk. And the other ninety-five percent of that code you have only a good guess where it's from, but you really don't know. Just how long do you think my career would last in front of either that bank inspector or my board of directors?"

Bob replied, nodding, "As a sales objection, that's as good as I've ever heard. I don't have a comeback to that one. You have a great day."

But Bob had inside information that the tech directors didn't. Several servers at the director's financial firm were *already running Red Hat Linux*. For example, a server administrator from the same company, many levels below the technology director on the org chart, would approach Red Hat's trade-show booth and buy a copy.

That server administrator was buying Red Hat Linux to satisfy a specific yet unbudgeted need. For example, an HR manager at his firm needed to send internal announcements, so would ask for help in doing so. If she didn't have $10,000 in her budget to buy the necessary software, the server administrator would suggest an inexpensive workaround—paying $49.95 to install Red Hat Linux that accomplished what she needed. Soon this growing demand for server applications became the norm, and Red Hat Linux's use in large corporations grew under the radar.

This story illustrates the grass-roots demand that Red Hat Linux both satisfied and created more of. Linux was an inexpensive, flexible, workable solution to major problems of corporate communications growth. Bob says situations like these later led to valuable corporate subscriptions because corporations like the one described above would later need to account for hundreds of Red Hat Linux applications running on their servers. They'd need to prove they had a license to use it, so ultimately they'd need support to keep Red Hat Linux up-to-date.

"And so many of Red Hat's very best customers are not the result of Red Hat's great salesmanship," Bob said. "They are the result of some new technology director discovering that he has a problem [accounting for] a thousand Red Hat servers, and his board is about to fire him because he has no control over these things." The upshot of this common situation was that many companies came to Red Hat, asking to buy the product—very nice work if you can get it.

So Red Hat positioned itself down the road to be needed by technology directors. Bob allowed the selling process to play out naturally, and didn't follow the conventional wisdom of forcing "top-down" sales on technology directors. It never would have worked in that type of corporate culture. He let the wave's energy do the work for him.

Red Hat Begins to Ride the Swelling Wave (1997)

Bob and Marc's hard work making Red Hat Linux easy to use was paying off. On February 1, 1997, when Red Hat had only twenty employees, it shared with Microsoft the honor of being *InfoWorld Magazine*'s product of the year for operating systems. In November that same year, *InfoWorld* published "Tired of NT? Put on Your Red Hat." It defined Red Hat as a "complete Internet server in a box for a price you can hardly turn down."[90]

Red Hat's marketing strategy was the linchpin of its early success. Through Vernon Leasing & Sales and *New York Linux* Bob had learned a great deal about marketing commodity products. He had been forced to figure out how to stand out in a crowd. He understood the importance of having a brand that stands for quality and service. Bob summarized Red Hat's marketing approach in a 2000 letter:

We looked at the commodity industries and began to recognize some ideas. All leading companies selling commodity products, including bottled water (Perrier or Evian), the soap business (Tide), or the tomato paste business (Heinz), base their marketing strategies on the building of strong brands. These brands must stand for quality, consistency, and reliability. We saw something in the brand management of these commodity products that we thought we could emulate....

Heinz does not own 60% of the market because Heinz tastes better....Heinz dominates the ketchup market because they have been able to define the taste of ketchup in the mind of ketchup consumers. Now the Heinz Ketchup brand is so effective that as consumers we think that ketchup that will not come out of the bottle is somehow better than ketchup that pours easily![91]

Like Heinz, Red Hat also excelled at marketing and Bob was open-source software's primary ambassador. The consummate salesman, Bob stumped free software to the media. He wasn't pushy as much as he was evangelical. His charm and witty metaphoric comparisons also helped Red Hat gain attention. For example, in speeches and interviews Bob compared proprietary software companies like Microsoft to "feudal lords."

And Red Hat spent considerable energy building a Web presence. They made REDHAT.com more than just a place to download Linux—it also became an online community for Linux users and developers. In addition, it offered other products related to open-source software, including a growing menu of downloads.

Now that Red Hat was getting more attention, it needed financing to keep up with demand. Venture capitalists started taking notice because Red Hat was a clear leader in the world of Linux. However, when Bob told them Red Hat's business strategy of giving away its software for free, they vanished.

"The VC's didn't understand because they weren't talking to the customers. Our business model hinged on giving away our software for free. And the VC's said, 'Well, you can't make money in the software business if you give your software away.' And I'd go, 'Well, that's too bad.'" Venture capitalists rarely called a second time, so Red Hat just went about its business of focusing on customers.

In 1996 Bob was referred to businessman Frank Batten, Jr., whose father, Frank Batten, Sr., was an early investor in the Weather Channel in 1981. From the fall of 1996 until August of 1997, Batten, Jr. observed Red Hat's unconventional business model make headway. Revenue ending February 28, 1997, had nearly tripled to $2.6 million from $930,000 the year before.

On August 15, 1997, Frank Batten, Jr. made a "Series A" $2 million investment in Red Hat by purchasing 6,801,400 shares for about 29 cents each. After the transaction, Bob and Marc each had approximately 4 million shares, making Batten, Jr. now its largest shareholder.

The Big Kahuna: Accepting the Wave's Energy (1998 and 1999)

Red Hat's biggest competitor was Microsoft, the same company that to get its own start had outfoxed IBM. The same company that was conniving to crush Netscape (and did). And by 1998, Microsoft was quite aware of Red Hat's taking market share.

Microsoft NT had the biggest market share for server operating systems, but its share wasn't growing: steady at 36% from 1997 to 1998.[92] In contrast, Linux-based operating systems were gaining popularity as its market share improved to 17% in 1998, from 7% in 1997.[93] And of the Linux servers shipped, 56% of those had Red Hat Linux, or approximately 9% of total new server license shipments. Of those 9% loaded with Red Hat Linux, a small percentage was actually paying Red Hat.

"The reality is most of our users don't pay us squat," Bob says. "So our business model [showed] that if we had millions of users, we only needed one-tenth of our users to actually find something of value to pay Red Hat for." But that small percentage was a growing part of a huge market.

Microsoft, on the other hand, was on the defensive. They didn't like Red Hat Linux invading their operating systems market. Did Microsoft feel threatened? "If Microsoft's earning $40 billion worth of operating system sales, and if we [reduce that to] a $4 billion-a-year market, because nine out of ten of the people that use our operating system aren't going to pay us, we're quite happy with a share of a $4 billion-a-year market," Bob recalls. "However, Microsoft cannot afford to change their business model, because they have $40 billion worth of sales to protect."

What could Microsoft do? How does a company beat free software—or free anything, for that matter? "The beauty of it is we knew they couldn't respond to us. There were barriers to entry from the big guys coming in," Bob explains.

Yet Microsoft tried to combat Linux in a surge of public relations. A Mindcraft, Inc. report showed that Linux was 2.5x slower than Windows NT. But thousands of Linux users refuted the report as bogus. When it was later shown that Microsoft paid Mindcraft for the report, the giant came away with egg on its face.[94]

To take advantage of Linux's growing popularity, in 1998 and 1999 Red Hat negotiated a whirlwind of product-integration, co-marketing, and distribution partnership deals with global software and technology companies such as IBM, Dell, Intel, Compaq, Oracle, SAP, Netscape, Hewlett-Packard, and Novell. Their customers were asking for a Linux solution. The big firms wanted to figure out a way to capitalize on Linux— or at least not miss out on its value to both their customers and employees at every level.

Red Hat was a $10 million company when doing these deals, but Bob was negotiating with these multi-billion-dollar companies practically as an equal because of Red Hat's unique business model and value proposition. Bob Young's co-authored book, *Under the Radar*, tells stories of intense negotiations. IBM Vice President Bob Dies once told Red Hat, "You need to understand we can just come in and take the market from you," then he backtracked, adding, "But we don't want to..." Red Hat walked away from IBM due to a contract disagreement over an indemnity clause, but IBM came back and resolved the issue.[95]

While negotiating with some of the world's most powerful companies, Red Hat never wavered from giving away its code for free. And the website was becoming a hub for Linux discussion groups, downloads, and applications. In March 1999, RedHat.com had 265,000 unique visitors and 2.5 million page views. With diligence and great patience, Red Hat had remained balanced on the wave, and those institutionalized habits of balance were paying off. Red Hat was hitting its growth inflection point.

During 1998 and 1999 Intel, Netscape, Benchmark Capital, and Greylock Management invested more than $13 million in Red Hat to support increased demand. In 1999 Red Hat's board wanted to explore taking the company public. The motivation wasn't just to raise capital, but also to gain credibility for Red Hat and Linux. The reasoning was that after going public, big companies that in the past had rejected Red Hat would reconsider them as a viable vendor. "Not until Red Hat went public did Linux become safe for corporate managers to invest in," Bob said.

Red Hat indeed went public, on August 11, 1999, and in the

midst of the dot.com boom. It sold approximately ten percent of Red Hat's shares, raising $84 million – or 6 million shares for $14 per share. The offering valued Red Hat at approximately $840 million—an enormous valuation, considering that revenue ending February 28, 1999, was only $10.8 million.

After Red Hat went public, operations grew more complex. Revenues ending February 28, 2000, increased to $52.8 million. And the upstart now had hundreds of employees spread out all over the world. Managing the many interrelated operational functions was challenging for Bob since he had never juggled competing interests to that degree.

"Red Hat had moved from this period where innovation was the #1 priority and process management was a secondary priority, to the opposite," Bob recalls. "It was blindingly obvious to all concerned that I was way past my pay grade. Which means I'd had no experience running a business as big as Red Hat had become."

Late in 1998, Greylock helped recruit to Red Hat 41-year-old Matthew Szulik. He was a seasoned technology executive with experience managing growth-oriented technology firms. Matthew had recently helped MapInfo go public. After arriving at Red Hat, Szulik was soon promoted to president and worked in that role for Bob.

In November, 1999, Bob turned over the CEO position to Matthew because he saw that managing Red Hat was beyond his experience level and that running a larger business was not work he liked doing. To this day Bob insists that helping recruit Matthew to Red Hat was his single biggest contribution to the success of the company. Szulik was able to keep the company, though now under all the pressures of public-company scrutiny, still surfing successfully.

Where is Red Hat now?

Red Hat has remained true to its open-source value proposition. As of January 17, 2017, its market capitalization was more than $13 billion. The company has evolved from selling $49.95 CDs to selling multi-year enterprise subscriptions and services. Red Hat is far beyond viability and exhibits plenty of strength for the future.

Red Hat's stock price has excelled, too. According to Morningstar, it has returned an average of 20.8% annually for the fifteen years ending June 15, 2016. For that same period of time, the S&P 500 has returned an average of 5.7% annually and the software application stock category has returned an average of 7.8% annually. Microsoft's return during that same period has averaged 3.9%.

According to an August, 2001, *New York Times* article, even Bill Gates has invested in Red Hat stock. "Most of Cascade's funds managed by Michael Larson on behalf of Mr. Gates are in Microsoft stock. The fund also holds stakes in Liberty Satellite and Technology, Inc. a company controlled by Liberty Media, and in the software company Red Hat, Inc."[96]

Bob remained on the Board of Directors at Red Hat until he retired in 2005 to pursue his new venture, Lulu.com. "In a funny way, my resignation is perhaps the finest compliment I can pay to everyone associated with Red Hat today; I have complete confidence in the future of the company," Bob told *eWeek.com* that year.[97]

Lulu, an "open publishing" company, has helped 1.1 million "creators" publish 20,000 books, CDs, ebooks, calendars, and other works of art per month. Bob was one of the first entrepreneurs to recognize self-publishing as a big opportunity.

Conclusion
In which surfing big waves involves more than just luck.

In 1999 35-year-old Mark Benioff, a Vice President at Oracle, started salesforce.com as a new type of customer relationship management (CRM) system. CRM is a multi-billion-dollar industry that helps businesses track customers, new-order pipelines, reminders, sales management reporting, and marketing campaigns. CRM was growing in popularity as a tool for businesses, but it was expensive and difficult to use. Benioff's goal was to "to make enterprise software as easy to use as a website like Amazon.com."[98]

Mark's idea was to apply a new kind of technology, software-as-a-service (SaaS), to CRM. SaaS is a software application that saves time and aggravation because it doesn't have to be installed on a computer—instead, the software and data are stored on a server elsewhere—the cloud. The application is delivered via the internet. Users log into the application's website and the application works. Their content is saved securely on a server – not on a computer that requires hard drive space. Another advantage of SaaS is that it creates a recurring revenue stream since customers often pay monthly fees for access.

When Benioff started Salesforce.com, SaaS was still in its infancy. But as did Bob, Mark sensed a cloud-storm brewing offshore that could bring big waves. CRM was the perfect application for SaaS.

But making salesforce.com a viable business with that unconventional business plan would be a daunting task because it had to take on an established leader: multi-billion CRM provider Siebel Systems. In order to compete, Benioff not only created an innovative delivery using SaaS, he also listened very carefully to his potential customers.

From a rented a one-bedroom apartment in San Francisco,

which they called their "Laboratory," Benioff and three software developers built the first prototype and tested it with dozens of salespersons to understand what the market really wanted. "We listened and then responded by designing salesforce.com to be all the things that traditional software wasn't," Mark writes in his book *Beyond the Cloud*. "Unlike the way software had traditionally been developed—in secret—everyone was welcome at the Laboratory.... Being inclusive of potential users from large and small companies across the world helped us gain valuable insight."[99]

Like Red Hat, Salesforce.com carved a niche early by selling to businesses that wanted CRM to be easy to use. They looked for customers who previously hadn't wanted to install complicated software by launching a marketing campaign called "No Software," illustrated by writing "Software" encircled in red and cut by a slash.

Benioff's plan worked. Salesforce.com's revenue rose from $5.4 million in 2001 to $96 million in 2004, the year it went public. And since then, revenues have increased to $6.7 billion in 2016. Benioff remains its CEO.

Salesforce.com successfully competed against Siebel Systems just as Red Hat successfully competed with Microsoft. According to Morningstar, salesforce.com has returned an average of 29.78% annually for the five years ending May 4, 2012. For that same period of time, the S&P 500 has returned an average of 0.64% annually and the software application stock category has returned on average 7.30% annually.

Was Benioff lucky because he was in the right place at the right time? Did a perfect juncture of time and place allow him to notice that SaaS could be applied to CRM?

And what role did luck play with Red Hat's ability to ride the wave of open-source software? Was Bob lucky or good?

Entrepreneurs create their own luck, Bob Young says. For

comparison, he cites his brother Michael, who has learning dis-abilities, but still manages invariably to win the family's annual fishing tournament because he keeps "lines in the water" by fish-ing longer hours than anyone else. The more you fish, the "luck-ier" you're going to appear to be catching fish. It's not pure luck. The top winners on Bass Masters prepare better, search better, and thus they attract the odds to their side better than the other guys."

Bob says, too, that entrepreneurs possess a certain degree of optimism that helps them keep lines in the water, keep pressing on, seeking balance—not tempting disaster. In sum, they try more ways to land fish. Bob says that the extra effort is often what makes entrepreneurs successful.

"What entrepreneurs have that keeps them going is an innate sense of optimism. It has to be innate. Because we're too dumb to give up. When everything is spiraling down out of control, you genuinely believe somehow, some way, some chance, you'll get lucky. The difference between success and failure is much narrow-er, and is much more chance-driven than people think—it's a very fine line between the two.

"The great quote for me is Vince Lombardi's idea that the harder he works, the luckier he seems to get. You know? Because you don't control luck. But the harder you work, the more you're putting the odds on your side; betting that good things will come your way."

Professional surfer Kelly Slater effectively says the same thing as Bob when he reveals his strategy for not drowning when surfing big waves. He knows survival can come down to chance, but he tries to attract luck to his side through taking on rigorous experi-ences and maintaining minute-by-minute calculations, not letting his awareness flag or be distracted by anything:

For me the answer is to be calculated about [surfing dangerous waves], especially when it gets big.... You have to ease yourself in; don't just get out there and paddle deep. What was the biggest wave that came in the last hour, and where did that thing break? What shape was it, compared to the smaller ones? When you're surfing an outer reef at twenty-five feet, you're going to need all those evaluations because it's going to break top to bottom. If you get caught inside, you need to know where to paddle to get to where the energy is dispersed more and you can get under it. It's all about calculations.[100]

Kelly doesn't leave survival to chance – instead he listens to the wave. And he pays very close attention to the wave's every characteristic so that he doesn't fail to know what's going on around him.

Isn't that what Bob did in building Red Hat? The reason Bob was successful is not only that he "kept lines in the water" but also that he listened carefully to customers, didn't treat them as profit-sources, and built his product around his receptivity to them—unlike his competition, who did things the same old way, by the numbers.

For example, if, back in 1991, Bob hadn't attended UNIX-user meetings while working for Greyvest in New York, he wouldn't have learned so early about Linux. Perhaps that was part of what my friend meant when he said Bob "was in the right place at the right time."

Bob created his luck in other ways. First of all, just showing up as an outsider to those "computer-wizard" meetings shows a will to learn and listen as an early stage of winning. When he first started attending those Unix meetings, the members made him feel uncomfortable, different from them. But he made himself relevant by publishing a newsletter for them, giving them something useful, paying attention, and earning their trust. And when Greyvest laid Bob off, he didn't go out and find a job just anywhere. He worked to make a business out of *New York Unix*. To earn a living,

Bob kept throwing lines in the water and listening—and learning. Then, while running *New York Unix*, he didn't go through the motions. Instead, he asked readers for niche content. That's how he discovered Linux in its infancy. And when Bob discovered Linux, he didn't stumble into Marc Ewing; he discovered Marc by asking customers who was making the best Linux programs. After he was directed to Marc, he went on a "tour" to figure out how to build a company that could compete with multi-billion-dollar companies like Microsoft.

That tour was how Bob came up with Red Hat's unconventional yet effective business model of giving away its product for free to some customers—then charging money for service and support for those who needed it.

Bob came to realize that listening to customers would be the key to Red Hat's success. "I saw an opportunity," Bob says. "I saw the benefit of open-source articulated by guys like Thomas Sterling at Goddard. What all the business guys working for Oracle and Sun Microsystems and Microsoft and all the rest didn't have the opportunity to see because they weren't asking the questions."

Thousands of programmers all over the world built Linux, but Bob figured out the best way to turn their work into a business that benefited everyone except Microsoft. And then he uncovered paying customers by understanding the requirements of conservative corporations. He learned that software cost wasn't their critical concern— they needed support, service, and official legal documents to construct a history of legal actions, a paper trail.

Red Hat's creation was an integrative process. There were many moving parts –changes to Linux, big companies making threats, and Microsoft breathing down their necks. But Bob juggled the variables and put the pieces together successfully. Most important, he listened to what customers wanted. That completed his pattern of coiled, balanced energy potential, identifying with and learning the wave so well that he nearly became one with it. Who can deny the power of personal receptivity?

"In hindsight everyone puts these value judgments on [my decision to start Red Hat.] 'It took guts. It took courage. It took brilliance.' It didn't take any of those things. All it took is practical. It's common sense. It's what you already know: listen to your customer. If your customer says, 'If you do this for me, I will continue to buy your product. If you stop doing this for me, I'll stop buying your product.' It doesn't take any guts not to stop doing that."

Bob Young and Mark Benioff didn't successfully compete against established leaders Microsoft and Siebel Systems, respectively, only because they were lucky or "in the right place at the right time."

Call Red Hat lucky, skilled, or whatever. It doesn't matter. Just like waves coming to shore, the Linux revolution was going to happen with or without Bob. But the fact is, he got on the wave and accepted its energy – working with it, not against it, he didn't fall off. He used his perception of the energy to find his own balance on the board. He stayed alert and worked with the flow.

"We were surfing the wave," Bob said. "We were not driving the wave. Our job was to balance ourselves on top of this wave. There were other guys who had surfed the wave earlier who fell off...."

Bob saw that the force of this business wave was much more powerful than he himself. Like a skilled surfer, he didn't fight the wave, but accepted the fact and form of its energy. Surfers embrace the wave's force by taking *earthly nature* into account: wind speed, ocean depth, and wave patterns.

Entrepreneurs embrace the wave's force by taking *human nature* into account: spending patterns, technology trends, and psychological dynamics. But whether surfing real waves or business waves, the winning strategy is to go with the flow, listen, be alert, and remain balanced. It's common sense to do so. It's practical.

Innovation takes time and suffering. No hockey stick-shaped revenue growth curve exists without a good idea and blade years work (ok, *occasionally* blade months). Prior to setting on developing an idea, though, most of the characters in this book experienced circumstances and/or possessed personality traits that made them *desire* to create good ideas. For example, Wes became tired of creating turnkey software solutions only to see others enjoy the fruits of his work. Bob finished at the bottom third of his class and believed, therefore, that the world was not "set up" for him. I myself saw that I'd never accomplish my goals by working for a big bank my entire life.

Not surprisingly, then, these good ideas solve a particular problem arising from the founder's experience of frustration or hindrance to his work goals. To fix the problem, the inventor objectifies his or her frustration into creation and other contributing actions.

The Blade Years tells several recent stories of how emotional frustration has been turned to action. LendingTree was created because Doug hated the bank's complicated mortgage process, so he figured out a way that customers filled out only one application. Graham dreaded seeing children die from drowning, so he fabricated an electronic device, SEAL Innovation, to prevent those deaths. Schedulefly came out of Wes's cumbersome process of building a weekly restaurant work schedule and his wanting an alternative. Red Hat came from co-founder, Marc Ewing's lack of money to purchase an operating system he needed to build a product. He found Linux too difficult to use, so he created an easier version.

First Research is the result of my frustration at having to go through a lengthy, roundabout process to prepare for a sales call. No one helped me speed things up, so I created my own industry reports. Then I was well prepared to sell bank products to my clients. Brian Hamilton saw that the process of making meaningful financial calculations was too manual and time consuming, so he automated it, calling his good idea Sageworks. iContact co-founder Aaron Houghton needed to find a less onerous way for his customer to send email reminders to her mountain-cottage summer renters so he figured out a repeatable shortcut for her via web technology.

But these problems weren't solved overnight.

Recently, while attending a banking conference, I heard a speaker discuss the subject of innovation within banks. Banks could become more innovative, he said, if their employees at every level learned to think differently.

As an exercise to encourage innovation, he asked the audience to break into groups of five and spend ten minutes designing a better grocery cart. After the brainstorming, each group announced its ideas: carts with store coupons, carts with better wheels, carts with maps of the store, carts with better children's seats, and so forth. The audience appeared satisfied, even elated with their collective ideas to make grocery carts better.

"See!" the speaker concluded. "You really *can* innovate. See how easy it is to do?"

The speaker's point had merit—encouraging the audience to think more broadly and deeply about how to deliver banking products to customers. But reading and analyzing the histories of LendingTree, Red Hat, SEAL Innovation, iContact, First Research, Sageworks, and ScheduleFly suggests that authentic and lasting innovative business ideas aren't created from ten-minute brainstorming sessions with strangers. Instead, making good ideas useful requires several years of trial and error, experimentation, investment of time and money, and building upon small successes. Innovation that sticks requires dedicated time and obsessive devotion to solving a problem.

Chapter 8
Evaluation

The Panel Study of Entrepreneurial Development II database includes 195 companies that consider their product "new and unfamiliar" and their company "first to market a new product or service." The study reveals that the average time from product development to first revenues is 16 months. The longest time reported in the study is 23.1 years!

The Blade Years's seven chapters show a similar variety of terms needed from product development until the first revenue is received. For example, iContact received its first revenue for email marketing software almost immediately. Likewise, Red Hat received revenue shortly after Marc Ewing developed his version of Linux Software. Revenue for these start-ups began fast, but came in small amounts. Both companies needed three to five years to finally get enough customers to hit a growth inflection point.

Consider Sageworks' start-up. Sageworks was dreamed up in the mid-1990s and incorporated as a real business in January of 1998, but Brian Hamilton confirms that his company really didn't "begin" until 2002. Brian puts his long journey into perspective by saying that, "Everything takes time. That's the hard part. It's taken me a long time to learn that. You think you come up with a great idea and people just buy it. [But that's not the case.] And now people are, like, 'Oh, yeah, that's a great idea!' And I'm like,

'Well, fascinating, because I didn't just push it out there and have a bunch of [people] start calling me'... I had a trickle. Starting a business is like creating a movement, you know? It starts slow..."

A start-up's early success is much more the result of the founder's ingenuity and will-to-succeed than it is his or her developing a business strategy and structured plans. The entrepreneurial stories in this book reveal that the founders spend *years* tweaking and improving before they turn their good ideas into businesses. For example, Brian Hamilton spent 18 months writing Sageworks' artificial intelligence after forecasting it would take 30 days to write.

"[Spending too much time planning] is just silly," Brian concludes. "You can't explain that to someone who hasn't started a business because they will think you didn't know what you were doing. Well, the fact is it's true. You don't know—you're just trying stuff. That's what [a start-up] is."

This book sets down hard truths about trial and error, experimentation driving success. Doug Ledba at first named his start-up Bankwire, then learned that that was the name of the Federal Funds Transfer System. So Doug adjusted, coming up with an original name, LendingTree. Wes Aiken, founder of Schedulefly, ordered $1,000 worth of product brochures after he started his business. Later he threw them away—wishing instead he'd bought a fishing rod. Graham Snyder spent six months and hundreds of hours building the first version of an anti-drowning device, and today he admits the prototype bears little relation to his present model.

When Ryan Allis first pursued iContact, he dropped out of college, optimistic he'd earn a million dollars his first year—only to sell $11,964 worth of software. And when banks wouldn't at first buy First Research, I attempted to sell it to high schools, only to be mocked by a sarcastic bunch of students who were showing me thereby that they were not the product's target audience. I'd have to adjust to reality, searching more effectively for that proper set of customers. Even the late Benjamin Franklin, who started a successful printing business, took a long voyage to England to buy printing equipment, only to find out halfway there that he had no credit or money to do so.

The takeaway from these start-up mishaps isn't that these entrepreneurs failed or had a temporary lapse of reason. Not at all. The takeaway is that these bumps in the road are expected when starting innovative companies. Mistakes are how you learn. These trip-ups are actually part of the creative process and provide new ideas that the founder wouldn't have had without the error. Furthermore, the recovery period generates new energy and direction—once you mop up the tears shed.

In order to endure a long period of creation-to-viability, entrepreneurs must deal with long periods of suffering, feelings of isolation, and fear of failure. Suffering does not mean lying around crying or feeling sorry for yourself. "To suffer" means "to endure pain passionately and willingly." Suffering of this kind is what the founder of a start-up expects and accepts while enduring the pain of adjusting to uncomfortable things that come with managing the first four years of a start-up. This kind of suffering is requisite before an entrepreneur produces results.

A start-up is often like a work of art – full of tweaks, throwaways, good ideas, bad ideas, and hard knocks. Ralph Waldo Emerson said, "Artists must be sacrificed to their art. Like bees, they must put their lives into the sting they give."[101] Like artists, innovative entrepreneurs sacrifice if they create with the proper focus and devotion to problem-solving.

The crux of the founder's dilemma is the daunting question: How long do I keep my doors open before hitting a growth inflection point? Or, how long should I keep fighting for viability? Three years? Five years? *Ten years*? Some ideas may never work well in business, no matter how long an energized founder keeps trying.

The answer to "How long should I fight? is a matter of feel. After years of trying, most founders have a gut instinct as to whether their idea is good enough for an adequate number of customers to pay for it. Early adopters normally provide most of the helpful product advice necessary to help founders make a decision.

Most founders who abandon their good idea give up too early, however. Based on the stories told to me for this book, it usually requires two to four years to hit a growth inflection point, not six to twelve months—the time cost that many entrepreneurs antici-pate when starting up.

Innovation takes longer than you think.

"An Entrepreneur's Riches Are His Hints"

In *Profiles of Genius*, author Gene Landrum writes that "The entrepreneur's riches are his hints."[102] Hints enable founders of start-ups to transform their *ideas* into *workable, well-designed, integrated products* that respond to customers' needs and desires. Each hint is like the missing piece to a puzzle, slowly discovered and put into the right slot to complete the whole.

For example, when starting First Research and unsuccessfully trying to sell to credit managers who handle a bank's information, I had this advice from a friend: "I'm not surprised credit manag-ers at banks aren't buying into your industry research report idea. Their nature and training make them risk-averse to new ideas. You should be selling to the sales leaders at banks." This one hint made a big difference in my eventual success in selling First Research to banks.

Tyler Rullman of Schedulefly said that early in the business's incubation, the founders needed to learn more about their prod-uct's efficacy: "We needed people in the system giving us feed-back because the product wasn't ready at that point." Efficiently translating that feedback into a better product was instrumental to Schedulefly's later success.

In every start-up the vital process of translating hints into a better product is, of necessity, a human, inefficient process—and that's one reason why start-up incubations are so long. The founder has to decipher hundreds of clues, balance conflicting advice, and translate these useful hints into tiny improvements, then check them thoroughly. The process of translating hints into action is, therefore, like putting together a 5,000-piece puzzle; it takes years. And the process can't be rushed—it has to take place naturally so that information about materials or data is communicated to all those involved—especially customers—in language they understand, and then integrated by them into their daily work habits before they can return the next stage of meaningful feedback.

Early Adopters are Difficult to Find

For our weekly "Family Night," my wife, two young children, and I often eat pizza, play board games, and end the evening with a movie and popcorn.

One evening we have an unforeseen hitch in the plan. The popcorn from our new bag and new brand won't pop. "Mommy, I think we bought a broken bag of popcorn," my daughter exclaims. "It's not popping!" Cue the tears.

I agree. The kernels have been heating in oil for what feels like forever. Can she be right? Is the bag of popcorn expired? Did we buy some bad kernels? I re-read the instructions. Perhaps the stove is too hot? Or not hot enough? Do we need to cover the popcorn? Are we using the wrong pan?

This is taking way too long, and family night is looking like a downer. Having popcorn with the movie is always to be the main event. I put the lid on the pan—that's my self-hint.

We wait and wait, all focused on the hot pan….

"Pop!"

"Yippie! It's popping, it's popping!" my son screams.

I'm surprised—I'd nearly given up.

But hold on. Several seconds goes by, not another pop. We're giving up again. It seems the one pop was a lucky kernel. That's all. But then we hear another pop … and a few seconds later another. Then nothing.

"Daddy! It's stopping again!" my son cries.

"Hang in there, kids, I think we might get popcorn after all." Truth is, I have a hard time believing that.

Finally, after an eternity, the popcorn begins popping again, "pop…pop…..pop….pop………….pop..pop..pop pop pop pop pop pop pop pop pop pop pop pop pop pop pop pop pop pop pop, pop, pop, pop, etc."

"Yea! YIPPIE! YIPPIE!" my daughter yells. "We have popcorn! It worked! It worked! I knew we could do it!"

From my own experience in starting First Research, trying to land our first sale was like popping popcorn. Getting reliable sales numbers took longer than I'd calculated—each new customer representing a random pop. The long delays between sales made me feel as if I'd done something wrong, or that my idea wasn't good though I had no proof one way or the other. My daughter and I thought my popcorn was bad, though we had no proof, either. But looking back on the experience today, I realize that my delays in getting sales were normal.

My brother-in-law, Brad, experienced similar delays when starting Local Eye Site. "In the beginning, I'd close an occasional sale, but they were never enough to pay the bills," he recalls. Each widely spaced sale excited him, but after a couple of quiet days, Brad felt like giving up again. This pattern went on and on, until he set out to try some new gambit for increasing sales.

A common misconception is that if an innovative idea is a good one, then buyers will quickly gravitate to the good idea: "If you build it, they will come." However, attracting customers fast rarely occurs, even for really good ideas like Red Hat, Lending-Tree, Schedulefly, and iContact.

Consider the difficulty that Sageworks faced finding early adopters of its product. When, in 2002, Brian Hamilton of Sageworks had finally discovered a market to sell to, CPAs and consultants, he'd call 300 firms to get one sale. Most call recipients couldn't initially grasp his good idea. "But why would I want to do that?" the CPAs would ask Brian. He'd try to explain, but most of the time he couldn't get through their risk-averse, conventional thinking to make the first sale.

All the businesses in this book experienced sales delays. It takes longer than you think to get sales—even for great ideas.

During those early months when the signs of success are unclear, to say the least, we want to be aware that what we have built here is a foothold, a beachhead that provides foundational strength and balance for later on when leverage is manifest. For example, here is a review of each story including how the founders escaped his Blade Years and revenue turned northward.

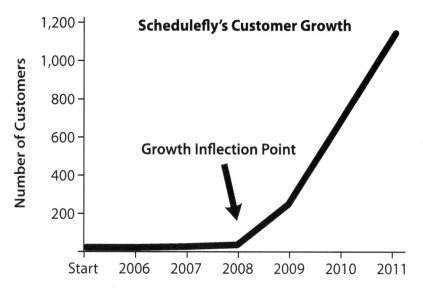

Schedulefly's Path to Success: Wes wrote the Schedulefly software in 2005 but nothing substantial happened to improve the product until 2007 when Tyler joined him and Wes started making product improvements. In 2008 the company's number of restaurant clients increased to 300 from 20 the year before. "I felt good about the email marketing," partner Tyler Rullman says, reflecting on 2008. "Not only did it put a lot of people in the product, we got a lot of good feedback and made a lot of great enhancements. We needed people in the system giving us feedback because the product wasn't ready at that point."

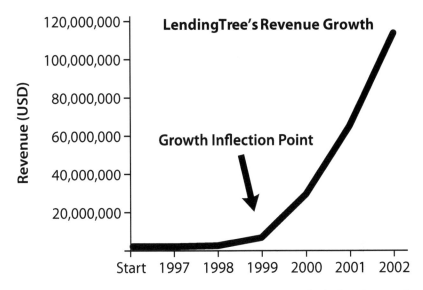

LendingTree's path: LendingTree's growth inflection point came in 1999. Doug Lebda had spent the company's first two years raising capital to build a technology application capable of transmitting data to and from banks. In 1998, even when it had a robust application, it struggled getting banks onboard to use its idea. But in 1999, it finally discovered repeatable methods that helped it grow faster. By November 1999 LendingTree had increased the number of banks in its network to ninety from fewer than twenty a year earlier. Its number of bank-closed loans increased from a few hundred in January 1999 to nearly 3,500 in August of that year.

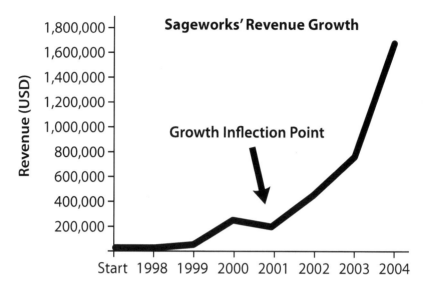

Sageworks' path – According to the graph above, Sageworks' growth inflection point could have occurred in 1999, 2000, or 2001, when it landed big accounts. But those accounts didn't result in *repeatable* activities, so revenue again flattened. Repeatable growth did occur in 2002, when Sageworks discovered how to sell to CPA firms. "When Drew joined, he started selling to individual CPAs," Brian recalls. "So our company really began in 2002." After Sageworks discovered its market, it started calling those potential accounts, constantly tweaking the message, and learning from the different outcomes. They soon learned how many CPA firms they had to call in order to get one order—one in three hundred in the beginning.

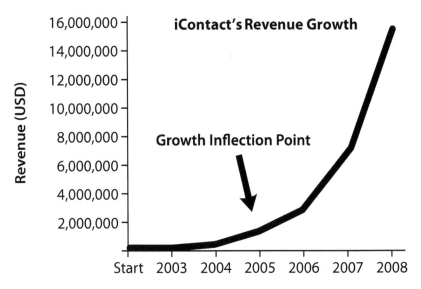

iContact's path – iContact's growth inflection point occurred in 2005, when revenue spiked to $1.3 million from $296,000 in 2004. Aaron told *Inc. Magazine* that iContact was able to show that its marketing was working. "The appeal is that the return from the cost-per-click model is predictable and scalable. By gathering data over several years, iContact was able to show that, for every dollar they put into marketing, they got back a customer who would spend a certain amount of money with them over a number of years." [103]

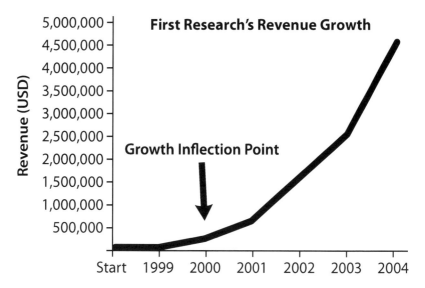

First Research's path: First Research's growth inflection point came in 2000, when its product and value proposition were fine-tuned to best meet consumer needs. That year it hired its third and fourth salespersons to repeat successful selling methods developed, then fine-tuned by Wil Brawley and Bobby Martin.

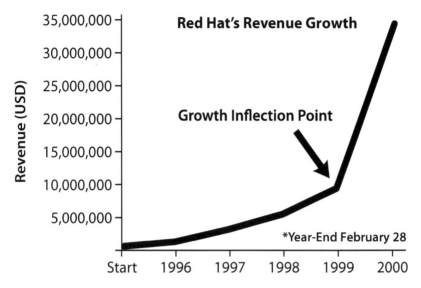

Red Hat's revenue growth chart with Growth Inflection Point arrow pointing to 1999, Revenue (USD) axis from 5,000,000 to 35,000,000, years Start, 1996, 1997, 1998, 1999, 2000. *Year-End February 28

Red Hat's path: Red Hat's growth inflection point came in 1999 when it went public. Before 1999, even though Red Hat's revenue roughly doubled each year, it was mostly selling individual CDs of Red Hat Linux. Its going public gave Red Hat the credibility to land large accounts with corporations—resulting in explosive growth. "[Corporate buyers] genuinely fought this open-source thing all the way through the nineties," co-founder Bob Young says.

Once a start-up hits its growth inflection point, it is learning to integrate its newly discovered business processes and carry them out smoothly. The start-up is then in a position to *prove that it can grow*. At this point, too, the risk for potential investors is smaller, and that start-up has a much greater chance of raising outside capital if the founder chooses.

The Blade Year's Paradox:
Success Requires Failure—Every Time

David Fleming's *ESPN Magazine* article "To Each His Own" examines hockey players' intimacy with their hockey sticks. "To a hockey player ‚sticks aren't equipment," he quotes Washington Capitals star Alex Ovechkin. "They are a piece of your body."[104]

Fleming says Bruce Boudreau, a star junior player in 1970s Toronto, customized his stick prior to matches. "Before games, the 20-year-old Boudreau would sit in his kitchen and customize the fiberglass curve of his weapon by carefully steaming it over a teakettle. Then he'd wedge it under a door hinge and bend it until it was perfect, race outside and plunge it into the snow to set the blade."[105]

Through tweaks and adjustments, Bruce Boudreau customized the *blade* of his hockey stick—the part of the stick that scores goals. The founder of an innovative business had best do likewise. For a start-up, the first three or four years, the "blade years," is the time period when founders gather and integrate important foundational knowledge. For example, during Red Hat's blade years founder Bob Young was earning very little money, instead making a "tour" of North America and learning that buyers desired control—not features. This hard-won, counter-intuitive knowledge became the foundation for what supported Red Hat's growth several years later.

The Blade Years may feel to the founder like his or her company is a house of cards—ready to fall apart at any time. These first years may not feel like good times, but the lack of early success doesn't mean that their idea is not viable. For example, what if Bob Young had given up after he failed for more than a year to gain distribution channels to sell Red Hat's software? Or if Tyler and Wes had quit during the twenty months they spent trying to find the best sales and marketing method, one that stuck? But they pressed on, trying and rejecting patterns and methods for more than three years.

Three years of withstanding perceived failure as the requisite impetus for success is a paradoxical law of founding an innovative business, but it's the truest formula for turning good ideas into viable companies. Why is this paradox so accurate? Because it's real and true to the start-up experience of founder after founder, seven of them documented here.

These seven stories show that the best methods, tactics, and strategies, the ones that propel their companies forward, come from trial and error—and more of the same—during the blade years. And it takes longer than you think!

Orson Welles' 1941 film, *Citizen Kane*, his first and the one considered to be his greatest, is inspired by the life of newspaper mogul William Randolph Hearst, a friend of the young Welles' father. The film's main character, Charles Foster Kane, is taken away from his parents as a young boy when his mother discovers a fortune's-worth of copper deposits on her Colorado farmland. Since the boy will inherit enormous wealth, his mother sends him to New York to be raised, and thus controlled, by a miserly banker, Mr. Thatcher.

When Kane turns 25 he returns from an adventure in Europe and is given control of his fortune by Thatcher. Instead of choosing to spend his time managing his vast array of investments, Kane chooses instead to run *The New York Inquirer*, a newspaper that is but a tiny part of his inheritance. He uses the *Inquirer* to expose crooked politicians, cheating financiers, union bosses, railroad tycoons—anyone who is out of line, in his opinion.

Mr. Thatcher, angry with the young man's choice to ignore managing his wealth for the opportunity to expose unscrupulous officials, many of whom are Thatcher's cronies, storms into

Kane's office and shouts: "Is THIS your idea of running a newspaper?!" Clearly, Kane's guardian despises the cheap shots his former ward takes at all these biggies—even though much of their abuse of the public trust is true.

Kane looks up at him and replies, calmly and wryly, "I have no idea of HOW to run a newspaper. I just keep doing everything I can think of to do!"

Kane's clever and candid retort is a precept for all innovative entrepreneurs to follow in turning our good ideas into profitable companies like his fictional *New York Inquirer*—an innovative newspaper for its time, the late nineteenth century. None of us, including myself, really understand at the moment of starting a venture *how* we will make our ideas successful, we "just keep doing everything [we] can think of to do."

Successful innovative start-ups of all sizes ascribe to this formula today. Whether we're Jeff Bezos starting Amazon by experimenting with how to best pack boxes to maintain accurate inventory records or Wes Aiken writing his Schedulefly software at home in his pajamas while he grows a beard over the weeks—the most successful entrepreneurs just keep trying things until they find processes that work. They often brave this period of "trying things" for three years or more.

Even so and despite the many challenges, this chosen life can become more than the fulfillment of the Chinese curse "May you live in interesting times." This "life-time" can, with dedication, brains, heart, sweat, and curiosity be shaped by a willing founder into a business that makes a real contribution, gives satisfaction every day he/she comes to work, and even begins to feel inevitable, the perfect choice of all.

Excelsior! Ever Upward!

Appendix

1 (The Police 1979)
2 (Drucker 1985)
3 (Gladwell 2008) p 40.
4 (Gladwell 2008)
5 (Sorkin 2010)
6 (Lowe 1979)
7 (Hansson 2010)
8 (Curtin 2008) p 211
9 (Wright 2007)
10 (Landrum 1993) p135
11 (Landrum 1993) p162
12 (Barenaked Ladies 1993)
13 (Hjelt 2001)
14 (Yang 2009)
15 (Schlender 2000)
16 (Schlender 2000)
17 (Arias 2009)
18 (Gilder 1985)
19 (Branson 2006)
20 (Strachan 2011)
21 (Manta 2012)
22 (Jean Teller 2012)
23 (Staff Reports 2008)
24 (Jean Teller 2012)
25 (Curtin 2008) p. 227
26 (Encyclopedia Britannica 2012)

27 (Encyclopedia Britannica 2012)
28 (Duckworth 2007)
29 (Houda 2010)
30 (Email Marketing)
31 (Dunbar 2008)
32 (Balboni 2007)
33 (Gladwell 2008)
34 (Branson 1998, 2004)
35 (Allis, 2008) p.27.
36 (Quinn 2010)
37 (Allis 2008) p.27
38 (Allis 2008) p.27
39 (Mendell 2012)
40 (The News & Observer n.d.)
41 (Allis, iContact & Vocus Combine Forces 2012)
42 (Brandt 2011)
43 (Brandt 2011) Location 996
44 (Brandt 2011) Location 827
45 (Brandt 2011) Location 853
46 (Brandt 2011)
47 (Brandt 2011) Location 943
48 (Chang 2011)
49 (Spingsteen 1984)
50 (Payscale.com 2012)
51 (Isaacson 2011)

52 (Stross 2007) Location 4710
53 (Stross 2007) Location 4711
54 (Stross 2007) Location 1345
55 (Drucker 1985)
56 (Gabler 2006) Chapters 1-4
57 (Gabler 2006) location 1229-35
58 (Gabler 2006) Location 1627
59 (Gabler 2006) Location 1573
60 (Gabler 2006) Location 1659
61 (Gabler 2006) Location 1698
62 (Gabler 2006) Location 2481
63 (Gabler 2006) Location 2507
64 (Gabler 2006) Location 2723
65 (Sartre 1952)
66 (Masur 2009)
67 (Reynolds 2008)
68 (Reynolds 2008)
69 (Raspe 1781)
70 (Alger 1962)
71 (Utley 1997) p. xiv
72 (Vries 1985) p. 163
73 (Gray 1937)
74 (Beckett 1954)
75 (Barrie 1987)
76 (Posner 1996) p. 29
77 (Perot 1996) p. 75
78 (Posner 1996) p. 30
79 (Posner 1996) p. 31
80 (Bear 1933) p. 38
81 (Bear 1933) p. 38
82 (Laver 1999)
83 (News Admin at Surfer Magazine 2007)
84 (Jarratt 2008) p44
85 (Economist 2001)
86 (Leonard 1999)
87 Funding Universe
88 (Mcguinness 2000)
89 (Rohm 1999)
90 (Hammond 1997)
91 (Young 2000)
92 (Rohm 1999) p.147
93 (Rohm 1999) p.50
94 (Rohm 1999) p. 146-147
95 (Rohm 1999) p. 48
96 (Bloomberg News 2001)
97 (Preimesberger 2005)
98 (Adler 2009)
99 (Adler 2009)
100 (Jarratt 2008) p.44
101 (Emerson 1904) p275
102 (Landrum 1993) p.165
103 (Quinn 2010)
104 (Fleming 2010)
105 (Fleming 2010)

Also by Bobby Martin

800CEO Read's Best-Selling
The Hockey Stick Principles now available on
Amazon and bookstores across the country.

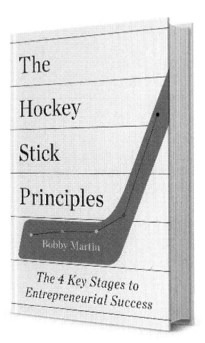

Learn more at BobbyMartin.me

Made in the USA
Columbia, SC
07 December 2020

26600463R00126